Takeout Training for Teachers

Group

Loveland, Colorado
group.com

Group resources really work!

This Group resource incorporates our R.E.A.L. approach to ministry. It reinforces a growing friendship with Jesus, encourages long-term learning, and results in life transformation, because it's

Relational
Learner-to-learner interaction enhances learning and builds Christian friendships.

Experiential
What learners experience through discussion and action sticks with them up to 9 times longer than what they simply hear or read.

Applicable
The aim of Christian education is to equip learners to be both hearers and doers of God's Word.

Learner-based
Learners understand and retain more when the learning process takes into consideration how they learn best.

Takeout Training for Teachers

Copyright © 2006 Group Publishing, Inc.

Visit our website: **group.com**

Credits
Contributing Authors: Sharon Carey, Teryl Cartwright, Lorie A. Erhard, Keith D. Johnson, Jan Kershner, Larry Shallenberger, Kristie Vosper, and Roxanne Wieman
Editor: Scott M. Kinner
Copy Editor: Deborah Helmers
Creative Development Editor: Mikal Keefer
Chief Creative Officer: Joani Schultz
Art Director/Book Designer: Greg Longbons/Coffee Bean Design Co.
Assistant Art Directors: Jean Bruns and Joyce Douglas
Illustrator: Mitch Mortimer
Cover Art Director/Designer: Josh Emrich
Cover Illustrator: Illustrated Alaskan Moose
Production Manager: DeAnne Lear

Library of Congress Cataloging-in-Publication Data
Takeout training for teachers.
      p.   cm.
   Includes index.
   ISBN 0-7644-3080-0 (pbk. : alk. paper)
  1.   Christian education--Teacher training. 2.   Christian education of children
   BV1533.T35 2006
   268' .3--dc22

                         2005023778

10 9 8 7 6 5   15 14 13 12
Printed in the United States of America.

Table of Contents

Lesson Preparation

Teachers will discover how to tweak lessons so every activity connects with their classes.

Personal Preparation

Teachers will get practical help preparing the most important part of any lesson—their own hearts.

Managing Expectations

Teachers will learn how to navigate expectations—and stay effective and motivated.

When Things Don't Go as Planned

Teachers will discover practical techniques to be ready for problems that come up.

Creativity in the Classroom

Teachers will learn how to creatively engage children and help kids learn the way they learn best.

Building a Relationship With a Child

Teachers will discover healthy ways to grow closer to children and become their students' trusted friends.

Leading a Child to a Faith Decision

Teachers will learn how to prepare kids for a life of following Christ.

Discipline in a Learning Environment

Teachers will learn ways to prevent most discipline issues and effective ways to handle any issues that do come up.

God Moments

Teachers will discover ways to find, grasp, and use teachable moments whenever they come up.

Evaluation and Reflection

Teachers will learn to evaluate themselves, look back on their successes and failures, and grow as teachers.

Introduction

Compared to the number of volunteers you *wanted* to have attend your last training session, how many *actually* attended?

The toughest part of teacher training is getting volunteers to actually *attend* training sessions. But that's nothing against the training you try to provide.

Volunteers hardly have time to attend training events. Your teachers are busy taking one child to soccer practice and another to a baseball game, helping their children with homework, attending PTA meetings, and preparing to lead a small group later in the week. And that could be in just one night!

And somewhere in that hectic schedule, your teachers have to figure out how to get some food into their families, too. The solution? Takeout.

Your teachers *love* to be trained, but there's no way a one-hour, sit-down training session fits into their schedules. So why not give them training in the same way they hunt their food? Takeout!

Just like takeout dinners, *Takeout Training for Teachers* is a quick and easy way to fill and energize your teachers. They may not be able to attend a training session, but even your busiest teachers can find 15 minutes to develop their skills while waiting for a child to finish up at soccer practice or for a PTA meeting to begin.

Takeout Training for Teachers focuses on challenges teachers report facing in classrooms like those in your church:

Lesson Preparation → Preparing lessons that are on target—all the time.

Personal Preparation → Preparing the most important part of a lesson—their hearts.

Managing Expectations → Navigating expectations—and staying motivated and effective.

When Things Don't Go as Planned → Being prepared for—and preventing—problems.

Creativity in the Classroom → Creatively engaging kids—all the time.

Building a Relationship With a Child → Safely and effectively building friendships with kids.

Leading a Child to a Faith Decision → Ideas for preparing kids to follow Christ—and celebrating with them when they do.

Discipline in a Learning Environment → Practical ideas for preventing behavior issues while at the same time maintaining learning.

God Moments ➜ Spotting moments God gives us for teaching—every time.

Evaluation and Reflection ➜ Learning from successes and failures—and from others.

You and your teachers get 52 training sessions, each one packed with specific, skill-building insights from master teachers.

And *Takeout Training for Teachers* is easy for *you*!

Each session comes in two formats: a reproducible two-page coaching handout and an electronic version on text CD that allows you to *make it your own* by placing the text in a newsletter, an e-mail, or even on your ministry's Web site. Edit and tweak it any way you'd like to connect with your teachers…in *your* church.

The audio CD contains 16 three-minute sessions in story form that present the qualities that make a good teacher a *great* teacher! You can make copies of this CD, record it into your ministry's voice-mail system—"press 2 for this month's Takeout Training for Teachers"—or get extra-creative and put it in audio form on your Web site.

And use the 12 energizing "E-couragements" to delight your teachers with e-mails they'll look forward to receiving.

Pick and choose from these training sessions, audio segments, and E-couragement clips, using them any way you'd like in your ministry. The sky's the limit!

Even if you already have great attendance at every one of your training events (if that's the case, you should start a consulting business), these resources will energize and encourage your volunteers!

Get ready for a tasty training treat. The takeout has been delivered and it's time to eat.

Enjoy!

Keith Johnson

A Position of Honor

> "Be strong and courageous. Do not be afraid or terrified because of them, for the Lord your God goes with you; he will never leave you nor forsake you" (Deuteronomy 31:6).

• How does this verse comfort you as you prepare to teach your first lesson?

• How can you be strong and courageous as you serve God in this way?

▼ Training Session

Congratulations! As a teacher, you're serving in a position of honor. You've been called—chosen—and with your curriculum in hand, you're ready to go.

If you're a veteran teacher, carry on.

But if you're new—to teaching or to your class—you may find a few butterflies in your stomach. That's OK…here are a few tips to banish those butterflies.

• **Pray.** Ask God to calm your nerves and use you to help children grow closer to him.

• **Prepare early.** Read the lesson early in the week. Gather supplies before Saturday night if you're teaching on Sunday. Run through the lesson several times—aloud. In front of a mirror, if that's helpful.

• **Ask questions.** Check to see that the supplies you're assuming are in the room are really there. Make sure they work. Talk to someone if you have questions about policies or procedures.

• **Arrive early.** This gives you time to make preparations that can only be made at the last minute. Plus, you can make sure the room is as you expect it.

• **Review guidelines and expectations.** If you're a new teacher, take time to establish guidelines and expectations. Setting two or three clear rules for your classroom will save you from conflict later.

• **Focus on relationships.** Learn names. Tell kids about yourself. Model the relaxed friendship you want children to have with each other.

Any lesson is improved when you've prepared, when you've prayed, and when you've practiced!

Take this training deeper as you think over these questions:

- What would a perfect day of teaching look like?

- What do you need to do to feel prepared and confident when teaching?

- If you were a child in your class, what would you expect from your teacher?

▼ **Journal**

Lord, my prayer for the next lesson I teach is...

The memories I want the children in my class to have are...

> Lord, bless me with confidence as I plan for and deliver my next lesson. Help me think of everything I need to make this next lesson effective. I want to be a light to your children! In Jesus' name, amen.

▼ **Application**

Set aside time in your calendar to prepare for your next lesson at *least* five days before you present it. If you develop this habit, you'll find more time to tweak the lesson and ask any questions you have well in advance.

The peace of mind is worth it!

The Recipe for Success

▼ Training Session

> "Preach the Word; be prepared in season and out of season; correct, rebuke and encourage—with great patience and careful instruction" (2 Timothy 4:2).

• What does "careful instruction" look like in your classroom?

• How prepared were you last week?

Remember the last time you bit into your dinner and thought, *That could have had a few more minutes in the oven*? Or maybe you've chipped a tooth on an overcooked charcoal burger?

Preparing a lesson is a lot like cooking. Underpreparing is dangerous: We end up reading the lesson from a script. It's unfocused and confusing. But overprepare and we lose nutritional value and taste: We've looked at the material so much that even *we're* bored with it.

Here's how to be sure to pop the lesson out of the oven right on time, every time:

• **Review your next lesson right after you teach the previous one.** You're already in your classroom, so check to see that the supplies you need are there. You're in teaching mode. Why not spend 30 minutes getting ready for next week?

• **Make Scripture covered in the next lesson part of your personal devotion time.** This is a good way to prepare your heart *and* your lesson.

• **If necessary, prepare in chunks.** Work on one activity a night. Gather your supplies during the week, and set them by your front door or in the trunk of your car.

It's never too early to start preparing, but it can *always* be too late.

As you prepare, though, remember it's possible to be *over*prepared. As silly as that sounds, it's true. You know you're overprepared when you've gone over the material so many times it's no longer fun and engaging.

You're overprepared if you can't imagine making tweaks or changes because the lesson is already memorized.

Prepare so you can be faithful to the content. But be sure you're having fun, too—that's what draws children into the learning experience.

The desire to overprepare is often a desire for control. Control is good, but so is spontaneity. Relinquish that control to co-teachers or student leaders. Let them prepare the sections of the class time they lead.

Enjoy the surprises.

And pray. Ask God to calm your nerves and guide you as you prepare.

Gourmet chefs spend years practicing and fine-tuning their greatest recipes. Find what works for you, and bam! you'll be cooking up effective lessons every time.

Take this training deeper as you think over these questions:

- Would you say your pace of preparation is a 1 (I wing it) or a 10 (I memorize it) or somewhere in between?

- What would you wish you could be most of the time, a little less scripted or a little more flexible?

▶ Journal

God, I tend to (circle one) a. overprepare b. underprepare because...

Help me to relinquish control to you in the area of...

You're dedicated. You're passionate about serving God and loving children. Add preparation to the mix and you have a recipe for success as a teacher!

▼ Application

Present one section of a lesson in front of a mirror. You'll get two things: an appreciative audience—yourself—and immediate feedback on how you look and act in front of children.

If you're prone to read your lesson like a script, you won't see anything because you're staring at your script. Practice looking at yourself in the mirror and only glance at the lesson when necessary. What do you notice?

If you're prone to overprepare, you may talk too rapidly or not pause for questions *and* answers.

How did this exercise help you?

Tailor-Made Lesson Fittings

▼ Training Session

"Then Saul dressed David in his own tunic. He put a coat of armor on him and a bronze helmet on his head... 'I cannot go in these,' he said to Saul, 'because I am not used to them.' So he took them off" (1 Samuel 17:38, 39b).

• What part of your life feels like you are wearing the "wrong outfit"?

• Why can't we fit into someone else's image or purpose for us?

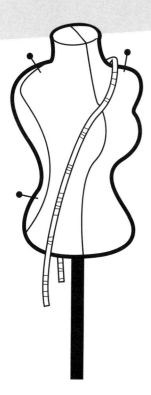

Just as David couldn't fight effectively in the wrong armor, we can't make someone else's lessons fit us perfectly.

We teachers love to try different ideas in our classrooms. But, as you know, alterations are required based on your personality and the way kids learn best.

Lessons about God aren't patterned after the latest fad—they're to be fashioned from unchangeable truth. If you want to make a lesson your own, first acknowledge that God owns the material.

Spend some time in prayer, asking God to use you to teach what he wants. You're special, and God chose you to teach. God *will* use your unique gifts and style to bring kids closer to him.

Don't be afraid to make a few tweaks and changes to your lesson to fit your abilities.

Maybe your lesson wants you to lead a worship song. But you're sure that your singing would cause kids to *not* be worshipful. This might be a good time to change the lesson so you have a student leader up front.

Another thing to keep in mind as you prepare your lesson: The only one who knows your kids is you! Your lesson might be heavy on teacher talk—and you're sure your kids can't sit and listen that long. Rework the teacher talk into group talk.

Finally, you can take it a step further in making it your own by adding personal examples and stories. Have your own example of not quite following God's directions? Tell that story as you teach about Jonah. You'll not only fit the lesson to your style, you'll give kids a glimpse into your life!

If you see that a lesson doesn't fit the way your kids learn or isn't engaging for your students, change it. We're teaching kids, not lessons. You have full permission to make it work.

Take this training deeper as you think over these questions:

- What does it take to make your lessons work for you?
- How can you teach for maximum impact?
- How can tailoring your lesson help your students learn?

▼ Journal

Lord, teach me to customize lessons by...

Tailor my life by...

Praise God for the gifts and experience he's entrusted to you to teach his children. You make a difference because you're part of the body of Christ. You are needed to teach as God has equipped you.

▼ Application

Make a list of the things you're good at as a teacher. Then look at your next lesson. Highlight (yes, it's OK to write in the book) the parts of the lesson that make those talents and gifts shine.

Then tweak an activity to make it work for you and your environment. Add a story. Reword the things you're supposed to say. Make it sound just like you wrote it yourself!

Winning Style for Each Child

▼ Training Session

"I have become all things to all men so that by all possible means I might save some" (1 Corinthians 9:22b).

_____

• Name two different ways God has taught you the same truth.

_____

• What does this Bible verse mean to your teaching?

One class, many kids, different needs.

Howard Gardner has identified at least eight different intelligences—ways kids learn—and there may be more! Chances are pretty good that each learning style is present in your class.

Some students want to learn by themselves (intrapersonal), while others learn best in a group (interpersonal). Some students learn best through words (linguistic), while others like to learn through movement (bodily-kinesthetic). Some use nature to learn best (naturalistic), some use logical skills (logical-mathematical), and some use art (spatial). Still others grow through music (musical).

A single activity in your lesson might not reach everyone, but how can you ensure the _lesson_ will?

Include activities from as many of the eight learning styles as possible. The good news: With a little planning, one activity can reach more than one learning style at a time.

Start by classifying your activities by the intelligences they meet. For example, if kids are working in groups to create a painting, that one activity would work for artistic learners and interpersonal learners alike.

Here are some more ideas to help you reach all learning styles:

• To learn more about learning styles, you can research Howard Gardner and his theory of multiple intelligences.

• If you are uncomfortable presenting a learning style (such as music or art), ask someone strong in this field to visit your classroom or give you suggestions.

• Don't be afraid to group kids together by learning style and allow them to learn the lesson in different ways. An artistic group could make a cartoon of a parable, while a musical group might turn that same parable into a rap.

It's important to present a lesson in a variety of styles to reach as many kids as possible. Everyone wins if you learn to base your lesson on your students' learning styles.

Take this training deeper as you think over these questions:

- What purpose does God have in creating us so we learn differently?

- How do you think your learning style influences your teaching?

- How can you integrate your kids' learning styles and your own teaching to make your lessons great?

▶ Journal

Father, let me be sensitive and learn how to...

Work in me as I become...

▼ Application

> **Teaching in different ways will show kids that you respect and appreciate their differences!**

Why not keep an "Eight Is Great" notebook? List ideas for activities by these categories: music, art, words, movement, logic, nature, interpersonal experiences, and individual activities. Keep in mind that one activity could go under several categories at the same time.

An idea journal helps when you need new ideas!

Staying Focused

> "Your word is a lamp to my feet and a light for my path" (Psalm 119:105).

• How important is the Bible in your everyday life?

• In what ways does the Bible influence the way you teach?

▼ Training Session

You're probably with your students about one hour each week. During that one hour, you compete for their attention. Their minds are likely focused on many other things: school, peers, soccer, video games, movies, piano lessons, television…the list goes on and on.

You don't have any minutes to waste, so it's critical you stay focused on God and your students, and that the lesson do the same.

Evaluate your activities. Take a ruthless look at every activity in next week's lesson. Is it teaching kids something new about God or just keeping them busy? Does each activity foster a real relationship with Jesus? Does it help kids see how to use their faith at school or on the playing field?

If there are more busywork activities than God-centered ones, you have work to do. *Every* activity needs to stay focused on a growing relationship with Jesus. Otherwise, you're just filling time.

Evaluate your own goals in teaching. Are you there out of duty? Because you like entertaining a crowd? Or because you want to help kids know, love, and follow Jesus?

Your personal goals for teaching will influence what you focus on during your lessons. Decide that your goal is to help kids know, love, and follow Jesus.

Remove obstacles. Want to help kids grow spiritually? Then be growing yourself. Read your Bible. Pray. Trust the Holy Spirit to guide you as you teach.

When your personal focus and your teaching focus are the same—to know, love, and follow Jesus—your teaching will be powerful!

POWERFUL TEACHING

Take this training deeper as you think over these questions:

- How much of your teaching is meat, and how much is busywork?
- What can you do to make your teaching more focused and streamlined?
- What can you do in your personal life to make sure you stay focused on God and his Word?

▼ Journal

*Lord, thank you for your Word, and for the Holy Spirit to guide me.
Help me to keep my teaching focused on you by. . .*

You have the most important job of all—teaching kids about Jesus! Don't let anything distract you from that worthy calling.

▼ Application

Write your own personal mission statement for your ministry. Tape it to the front of your teaching book, or frame it and hang it on the wall in your classroom. Read it before every class you teach. It will help you stay focused on the most important thing—Jesus!

Tell Me Again— Why Am I Doing This?

"Now it is required that those who have been given a trust must prove faithful" (1 Corinthians 4:2).

• With what gifts and skills has God entrusted you?

• How does your individual ministry to children declare faithfulness?

▼ Training Session

When you look out over a classroom full of squirming children, do you ever hear yourself saying, "Tell me again why I'm doing this?" Were you excited to volunteer for this ministry, or were you begged mercilessly until you agreed to take on a class—and now you're stuck?

There are many wonderful reasons to teach kids, but guilt and obligation are not on the list. Guilt may prod you along, but it will never empower. Ask yourself the following questions. Be honest with your answers.

• **Test your motive.** Ask yourself, "Do I *want* to teach?" Children need and deserve to be taught by someone who enjoys being elbow-to-elbow with them around a kid-size table. A good teacher says, "I choose to be here." But a great teacher says, "I *want* to be here."

• **Listen for your calling.** Ask yourself, "Am I called to teach?" Having a spiritual gift for conveying the truth of Scripture in a way that brings about change is God's way of telling a teacher to go teach. To stay the course in children's ministry (or any ministry), you must have a sense of calling from God. Without it, the weekly task of presenting God's truth in fresh ways becomes burdensome. Discover your spiritual gift and put it to work.

• **Examine your heart.** Ask yourself, "Do I have a servant attitude?" Teaching is largely about serving. Kids require our time, attention, and patience, and are able to give little in return. If your stamina for servanthood is low, you will not likely fill it with a classroom of attention-seeking 5-year-olds. Without a servant's heart, the privilege of helping kids know God turns into a duty and teaching becomes a task.

In a perfect world, only gifted teachers who thrive on crayons and lesson plans end up in front of a Sunday school class.

In the real world, however, you may find yourself teaching because there's a need and no one else to fill it. If that's your story—bless you for your willingness to serve. Continue to pray for God to use you in the way he sees best and to give you a heart for teaching.

Whether in teaching or helping behind the scenes, the opportunity to have a part in pointing children to God is a gift in itself. Use it to the best of your ability.

Take this training deeper as you think over these questions:

- If you wore a T-shirt that said, "I teach because _____," what would be written on the line?

- What has God shown you to be your spiritual gift?

- When you look out over a group of kids, what goes through your mind? How does that reaction help you know whether or not teaching is your strongest avenue of service?

▶ Journal

"…and that's why I teach."

Teachers don't teach because they have to, they teach because they can't help it. If you are called, gifted, and motivated by a desire to serve, God has a group of kids waiting for you with open arms. Go get 'em.

▼ Application

If you believe God has gifted you with an ability to teach, but are not happy in your present area of ministry, you might consider other avenues through which you can serve—but don't give up.

Take out five index cards. On each card write a reason you can't give up working with kids. Place each of the cards in a visible place, such as in your Bible, on a mirror, or in your car. When you see the cards, ask God to empower you to do his work in reaching children.

Do You Know What Your Job Is?

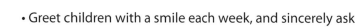

"So whether you eat or drink or whatever you do, do it all for the glory of God" (1 Corinthians 10:31).

- How can you ensure that you're doing everything for the glory of God?

- How does your ministry reflect this verse?

▼ Training Session

Teaching doesn't begin when the first child walks into your room and end when the last child leaves. Teaching is more than leading discussions, directing craft activities, and helping kids. And it *certainly* isn't just about standing in front of a room and talking to passive children. Do you know any passive children? They're *active*. And so is teaching.

Since teaching is an active job—and an important one—you need to know what's expected of you. And it's best to have those expectations in writing so you can refer to them again and again in the future. You need a ministry description. This simple piece of paper tells you what you're supposed to be doing. It's designed to lay out the goals of your position and the details of accomplishing those goals.

For example, one goal would be building lasting relationships with children. Your ministry description could list some steps you should take to ensure that goal is accomplished.

For instance, you could

- Greet children with a smile each week, and sincerely ask how each child is doing.

- Keep lines of communication open between yourself and each child you minister to by calling or sending a note at least once per month.

- You could also contact each child's parents every quarter to compliment their child and thank parents for letting the child continue to be involved in your class.

Having clear goals and suggestions laid out in a ministry description helps you meet the expectations of leaders in your church, as well as build expectations for yourself. Ask your leader if you have a ministry description. If not, ask for one. It's essential to your success. If your leader isn't sure where to start, jot down a few ideas to start the process.

Already have a ministry description? When's the last time you read it and prayed about how you're doing meeting the goals?

Take this training deeper as you think over these questions:

- What's the mission of your ministry position?
- How can you fully understand what you're supposed to be doing?
- How might having a ministry description help you?

▶ Journal

Give me wisdom as I . . .

Lord, help me live up to the expectations that . . .

God is using you to bring children into a close relationship with Jesus. No other expectation rises above this high calling. Thank you for serving to meet this goal!

▼ Application

Imagine you're suddenly unable to teach your class for five weeks. Will your replacement know what to do?

If *you* were to replace you, what would you want to know?

Maybe you're moving to a different type of ministry position after this year and you need to train your replacement. How would you do it? What would you tell that person? Without looking at a current ministry description (if you have one), write a ministry description that would help train your replacement.

Transferring DNA

▼ Training Session

"Therefore, since we are surrounded by such a great cloud of witnesses, let us throw off everything that hinders and the sin that so easily entangles, and let us run with perseverance the race marked out for us" (Hebrews 12:1).

• What kinds of things hinder you from teaching with perseverance?

• Think about the names and faces of some people in your "cloud of witnesses." What do you want them to witness?

All living things are filled with cells that grow and multiply. And it's the DNA inside those cells that determines the characteristics and structure of the living things. When the DNA is healthy, the organism is healthy. When the DNA is damaged, there can be some health or structure problems.

We are all cells in Christ's body. And we carry important DNA to transfer to the younger growing cells—our children. We have to do what we can to keep that DNA healthy and nourished.

However, when we hold on to sinful habits our spiritual DNA is damaged. Sin mars our character, and if we aren't careful we'll transfer our flaws onto the children we work with. For example, if you have an anemic prayer life, it's impossible to transfer a vital prayer life into your students. If you harbor bitterness against someone, you can't transfer the "joy DNA" to your students. That's frightening.

But it's a great thing that God is forgiving. He invites us to confess our sin and promises to heal our brokenness so he can create a new work in us. As God repairs our spiritual DNA, we become more effective teachers. We have a higher-quality spiritual DNA to transfer.

We don't need to be perfect people in order to teach. If that were the case, there would be no teachers. But we do need to be people who are quick to turn to God with our shortcomings.

Hebrews 12:1 suggests that the spiritual health of your children will grow with these things in your life:

• **You live your life as if children are watching.** Because they are. They're the "cloud of witnesses." There's no such thing as privately struggling. The quality of our spiritual DNA matters to everyone around us.

• **You quickly confess your sins to God and set your heart on following him.** This is where you "throw off everything that hinders."

• **You follow Christ in every aspect of your life.** By doing this you strengthen your own DNA so you can transfer healthy DNA to your children. This is how we "run with perseverance."

Take this training deeper as you think over these questions:

- Why do we tend to think that our struggles with sin are a "private matter"?
- How can you make repentance a more regular part of your friendship with God?
- What parts of your friendship with God would you like to transfer to your children?

▼ Journal

Lord, I need to confess...

Lord, help me build these spiritual qualities in the lives of the children I work with:

God has promised to complete the good work that he began in you! He knows your limitations and provides the grace to make up the difference!

▼ Application

Make a list of the parts of your friendship with Jesus that you would like to pass on to your students. Next, list the parts of your friendship with Jesus that need to be repaired before you can pass them on.

Take a moment in prayer to thank God for how he has helped you mature in your friendship with Jesus. Talk to God about what it would look like to repair your spiritual DNA and what you will do to make that happen. Ask God to continue to transform you with Jesus' spiritual DNA.

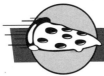

Organize Your Life for Classroom Success

"Therefore, prepare your minds for action; be self-controlled; set your hope fully on the grace to be given you when Jesus Christ is revealed" (1 Peter 1:13).

• How can you best prepare your mind and life for teaching?

• What changes might you need to make in your personal life in order to feel better prepared to teach?

▼ Training Session

We all agree that it's a worthy goal to have our minds prepared for action, ready to help children focus on the grace of Jesus. But that's not always how it works every week.

The reality is that some weeks the car won't start, the cat will throw up, you'll spill coffee on your shirt, or getting your kids ready will take a little longer than usual.

Those are the things that try the patience.

Then there are money concerns, family issues, marital discord, health problems, or stress at work.

Those are the things that try the soul.

No matter what, we're each expected to show up with a smile on our face, a spring in our step, and a life-changing lesson in hand. Realistic? You bet! (OK, maybe not always the spring-in-the-step part, right?)

But because we have God on our side, ready and willing to change our hearts and conform our spirits to his, we *can* come into class already victors!

God wants us to succeed in our ministry. He put us there. He knows the challenges we face. He wants to help. All we have to do is turn to him. Ask God to prepare your heart for his ministry, and he will.

In addition, there are a few practical steps you can take to help minimize the stressors in your ministry:

• **Get things ready the night before.** Set out the kids' clothes. Set the coffee maker so all you have to do is flip the switch. Put your teaching supplies by the door.

• **Ask for help in your church.** Make sure you have the assistance you need, both in and out of the classroom. Maybe there's someone who could shop for your supplies or make the copies you need. It doesn't hurt to ask.

• **Don't expect perfection**—of yourself or of your students. Not every week will be filled with earth-shattering teaching. Do your best, and let the Holy Spirit take care of the rest.

Rely on God. He won't let you down.

Take this training deeper as you think over these questions:

- What are the biggest stressors in your ministry?

- What can you do to eliminate the distractions in your ministry?

- How can you rely more on God?

▶ Journal

Lord, here are the stumbling blocks in my ministry. Please help me with…

Lord, bless me with self-discipline and commitment to follow through with…

Remember that God is with you. Turn to him for refreshment and renewal. Everyone needs that, especially in ministry. Satan will try to hamper you, but he won't be able to because you'll be relying on God.

▼ Application

Make a list of three action steps you'll take to minimize the stressors in your life and ministry. Take those action steps within the week (or you never will).

For example, you could start with this list:

- Get up 30 minutes earlier (and go to bed earlier) before I teach my next lesson.

- Write a list of my classroom and lesson needs to go over with my ministry coordinator.

- Spend a few minutes meditating on God's Word before I teach.

Then ask God to help you rely on him as you prepare your mind for action, gain self-control, and set your hope on the grace of Jesus.

'Sasperated

> "Immediately Jesus made the disciples get into the boat and go on ahead of him to the other side, while he dismissed the crowd. After he had dismissed them, he went up on a mountainside by himself to pray" (Matthew 14:22-23a).

- After a busy, stress-filled day, why do you think Jesus went off to pray?

- What do you do to ease your own stress that seems to work the best?

▼ Training Session

Three-year-old Christopher had a teacher who persistently exhibited extraordinary buoyancy and fortitude. This was remarkable because, let's face it, preschoolers can be tough on even the longest-tenured teacher.

Little Christopher was no exception.

One day after Christopher did a wonderful job of being tough for his teacher, he came home and reported to his mother, "Miss Becki was 'sasperated today!"

This wise teacher, rather than hiding her own frustration, actually shared with Christopher that she was *exasperated*. How did this wise teacher keep her down days out of the classroom?

She accurately measured her own emotional vulnerability for that particular day and shared it up front.

Having a bad day? That's OK. Everyone does every now and then, but your kids don't need to experience it, too. It's unfair for us to take our emotions out on children when we're experiencing something they aren't really the root of.

Miss Becki realized she was a little stressed-out, so she shared her feelings with her students. This type of self-disclosure goes a long way to creating an atmosphere of honesty and integrity.

But that's merely one way you can spare kids from your 'sasperation. Here are some others for you to consider:

• **Breathe.** Try this simple breathing exercise. Inhale for five seconds. Hold your breath for five seconds. (Count in your head— you're holding your breath.) Then exhale for ten seconds. Do this three or four times, and you'll find yourself clearly calmed and quietly centered.

• **Take some time for yourself.** Get your mind off what's bugging you. Take a long shower or bath. Curl up with a good book on the patio or in front of a cozy fire.

• **Pray.** Prayer is a great peace-producer! Give your situation to God. He asked us to (see Matthew 11:28).

Jesus went off to pray when he was having a bad day. Find what works for you to mentally, emotionally, and spiritually prepare to be an effective teacher no matter what kind of day you're having.

Take this training deeper as you think over these questions:

- When have you let your emotions take over in front of children? What happened?

- What can you do to keep your down days backstage?

- How would you confront a teaching partner who's having a bad day?

▶ Journal

Prayer was Christ's way of dealing with a stress-filled day.
List the types of things Jesus would have asked God about after his long day of feeding the 5,000.

How are these insights or prayer topics relevant to your own in-class or out-of-classroom stresses?

Prayer is God's way of taking our burdens off our hearts and into his arms. Stress ultimately has a spiritual solution! You can unload now!

▼ Application

Laughing, exercising, reading, reflecting, and singing are ways our bodies recharge and remove stress! Choose one activity this week that would provide one of these stress-eliminators. Here are some choices, or you can make up your own:

- Ride a bike.
- Take a walk with a friend (or pet).
- Read a novel.
- Sing in the shower.
- Take a long bath.
- Watch your favorite comedy on TV.

Teaming Up With Parents

> "Train a child in the way he should go, and when he is old he will not turn from it" (Proverbs 22:6).

• How well are your students spiritually nurtured at home?

• What are some things you're doing to work with parents in the spiritual growth of their children?

• What do parents expect of you?

▼ Training Session

Imagine you've done your family's grocery shopping for the week. You prepare one meal for your family, then padlock the pantry and fridge. "That's it," you tell your family. "See you next week."

Not much of a strategy for a healthy family, is it?

The Bible lessons you teach give the kids in your class a wonderful dose of nutrition—but it's just a single meal. You may be assuming the children are being fed at home, too—enjoying exposure to Scripture and being involved in spiritual discussion.

But is that really happening?

Some parents believe that what you provide in class is enough for their children to have a growing relationship with Jesus. Just as these parents send their kids to piano lessons for instruction, they send their children to you for spiritual instruction. You're the expert.

What do the parents of children in your class expect of you? Unless you ask, you have no way of knowing—it's just assumption. You won't be able to help those parents embrace their roles as the primary faith-shapers of their children until you learn what they expect.

Try some of these tips to identify what parents expect of you, and to clarify what your respective roles are in the faith development of their children.

• Ask parents to meet with you and set some specific spiritual goals for the coming year. Two or three goals will be enough. Identify what the parents will do—and what you'll do—to help children achieve goals.

• Encourage parents in their roles as the primary faith-shapers of their children. Watch reactions. Is this a role the parents want?

• Invite parents to be guests in your classroom so they can see what you do and don't do.

• Make home visits to each family represented in your class.

• Be approachable for parents. Ask parents how you can pray for them.

Your teaching has a powerful impact in the lives of children…but you can't do it all. Be sure parents have realistic expectations of your spiritual leadership in their kids' lives—and of what God expects of them.

Take this training deeper as you think over these questions:

- What do you think parents expect of you? How do you know?

- What areas need improvement as you work with parents?

- How will your students benefit from better teamwork between you and their parents? How will you?

▼ Journal

My prayer for my students' parents is...

Lord, as I team up with parents, help me...

Parents may not always express their gratitude for what you do for their children, but most have deep appreciation for your tremendously valuable influence. On behalf of all parents, thank you for all you do for God's young ones. Kingdom work is forever! Your efforts are everlasting!

▼ Application

Set up individual team-building sessions with the parents of each of your children to take place within the next month. Do these three things at the team-building meeting:

1. Set up spiritual goals to work on with their children. These should be goals that you have to work together to accomplish.

2. Develop a plan to be worked on both at church and at home.

3. Set check-off steps so you and parents know if you're meeting those expectations.

Entertainment Expectations

"Whatever you do, work at it with all your heart, as working for the Lord, not for men" (Colossians 3:23).

• Why do you teach?

• How would you define your own ministry style?

• What do students expect of you?

▼ Training Session

Kids *love* to be entertained.

Everything in their world is fast-paced and readily accessible. Kids are surrounded by televisions, CD players, computers, e-mail, cell phones, text messaging, and MP3 players. Even very young children are fed a diet of fast-paced visual entertainment.

Now think about church. And about teaching biblical concepts like patience, humility, and prayer.

It's not surprising that when your stimulation-saturated kids hear, "Be still and know that I am God," you see some confused looks.

As a teacher you probably don't have the latest technology or a Hollywood budget. But you do have something kids can't find anywhere else—the Truth…and yourself.

As you're genuine and vulnerable with your students, you'll develop a trusting relationship with them. As you depend on God, he'll guide your ministry and create opportunities to connect with kids.

If you're careful to make your ministry creative, engaging, relevant, and fun, kids *will* be engaged—and entertained! And they'll discover they can be friends of God!

Take this training deeper as you think over these questions:

- What do your students expect of you?

- How realistic are those expectations?

- How can you meet kids' expectations and still supply solid Bible teaching?

▼ Journal

Lord, please help me remember the real goal of my ministry.
Help me to focus on what you expect by...

Thank you for teaching. Thank you for stepping up when others decline. Thank you for being the one who tells kids about Jesus.

▼ Application

Write your description of a perfect teacher. What would that teacher accomplish? And how? How does that perfect teacher entertain as well as teach truth? How important is entertaining to you as you connect with kids?

Aligning With Your Church's Expectations

"You must teach what is in accord with sound doctrine" (Titus 2:1).

• What does your church expect of you as a teacher?

• What are the benefits of understanding your church's expectations as you teach?

▼ Training Session

Some churches expect their teachers to keep kids busy while parents are in "big church."

Other churches expect kids to be able to write a doctoral thesis in theology by the time they graduate sixth grade.

Most churches fall somewhere between the two extremes.

Do you know what your church expects of you as a teacher? It's critical that you do. It's hard to do a good job if you don't know what's expected of you.

Make sure you know the mission statement for your church's children's ministry. Don't have one? Encourage your children's pastor or director to put one together. You could even volunteer to help out with this!

Everything you do should fit under this mission statement. If it does, you're on your way to living up to your church's expectations.

It's also a good idea to ask as many questions as possible. Find out how much flexibility you have to apply your own style and creativity in your classroom. The good news: There's *plenty* of room for creativity!

Some questions you might ask are:

• Who's my go-to person when I have a question or concern?

• How loud can my class get when we enjoy learning experiences?

• What supplies will the church provide? What should I contribute?

• May I decorate my room any way I choose?

• If I'd like to change something, what's the process for making a suggestion or request?

Knowing the answers to these starter questions will help you begin to align with the church's expectations of you as a teacher. Then you can move on to the really important stuff: building relationships with children and helping kids grow closer to Jesus!

Take this training deeper as you think over these questions:

- How do you think fully understanding your church's expectations of you can positively affect the children in your class?

- What are the next steps for you to take to know what's expected of you as a teacher?

- How can you pray for your ministry's leaders—the people who set expectations of teachers?

▼ **Journal**

My thoughts of what my church expects of me are...

Lord, help me to follow your will as I...

Lord, thank you for letting me serve you, my church, and my students. Help me be faithful in meeting my church's expectations of me as a teacher. Even more important, help me meet your expectations. In Jesus' name, amen.

▼ Application

Meet with your leader and discuss the church's expectations in person. Bring your list of questions, suggestions, and concerns, and share your desire to make your classroom a success. Also, be sure to express your willingness to meet reasonable expectations.

Be a T.O.P. Teacher

Is there a verse that's guided your life? Write it here. If you can't think of just one verse for your life, choose a favorite passage.

_____

_____

_____

_____

_____

_____

_____

• Why has this been a key verse in your life?

_____

• How important is having a spiritual goal for yourself?

_____

• What do you expect of yourself as a teacher?

▼ Training Session

Why do you serve in children's ministry?

Why not sing in the choir? Or work as a parking lot attendant? Or simply fill a spot in a pew?

What is it about your role that captivates you to the extent that you'll prepare lessons, endure a child's temper tantrum, and miss "big church" on a regular basis?

Some serve out of guilt…or an inability to say "no" when asked.

But others serve in children's ministry because they're engergized by the challenge to create an environment that's engaging, encouraging, and enriching. They love helping students discover how to love, honor, and cherish Jesus.

No matter how you're serving, serve so you're a "T.O.P." teacher.

• Be **Tremendous** by trying something new each week. Set the bar high for creativity—as you stretch you'll keep students engaged and enthused! By the way, _tremendous_ doesn't mean _perfect_! Don't set the bar _too_ high. Know your limitations.

• Be relational with **Others** by intentionally getting to know students. Get on their level and enjoy a healthy relationship with kids!

• Be **Persistent** in your efforts! Never settle for being mediocre or average! You can make the hour students are in your class a remarkable hour—an amazing, God-infused, empowering time!

In a world of big people who seldom notice children, you stand out as remarkable because you're a T.O.P. teacher!

Take this training deeper as you think over these questions:

- Who do you ask to make sure you're reaching your goals?

- How are you a different person this year compared with last year?

- What will be the feature that will improve in your life NEXT year?

▶ Journal

*Spend some time filling in the blank in the following sentence
with as many nouns as you can think up:*

Lord, I need _____ to draw closer to you as a person and as a teacher.

Thank you for striving for the T.O.P. Set the bar for yourself high. Children deserve for you to be the very best you can be.

▼ Application

Write down the name of each child in your classroom. Beside each name write one goal that you have for that child to accomplish this year. Make sure it's related to what you have control over or what you can influence in your classroom. It could be to share toys or sing at least once—a lofty goal if you have a group of fifth-grade boys!

A+ Thou Good and Faithful Servant

"The Lord does not look at the things man looks at. Man looks at the outward appearance, but the Lord looks at the heart" (1 Samuel 16:7b).

- What do those around you observe as they watch you minister to children?

- What does God see when he looks at your heart?

▼ Training Session

This Sunday your pastor may not be watching you. Your children's ministry leader may not evaluate your lesson content. You may not have parents checking to make sure you taught their children well.

But remember that even though others might not be watching, God is. And it's his evaluation that counts most.

Maybe knowing that God will evaluate how faithfully you've used your gifts in service makes you nervous. You're painfully aware of your failures. You know your inadequacies. You wonder if you're making a difference.

But awards and applause are misleading. God is less impressed by the outward signs of accomplishment and a perfect performance than by your heart. God approves when we depend on him. And when we're faithful.

Here's how it works: We rely on God, and he gives us what we need to serve him effectively. We pray for his work to be done, and he gifts us. We learn his Word, prepare, confess, and pray, and God uses us in a specific place of service.

God commands our obedience, requires our sacrifice, and demands our holiness. Those are tough standards. With Jesus as our example, the grading curve is high.

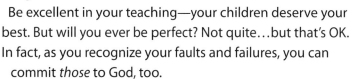

Be excellent in your teaching—your children deserve your best. But will you ever be perfect? Not quite…but that's OK. In fact, as you recognize your faults and failures, you can commit *those* to God, too.

Our weakness yielded to God's strength is a powerful combination. So don't worry about being a perfect teacher—you aren't. You never will be. But you *can* be faithful—and have fun in serving God!

Take this training deeper as you think over these questions:

- How can you rely even more fully on God?

- In what specific ways can you improve the way you serve God by focusing less on performance and more on dependence?

▼ Journal

Picture the dust finally settling around the edges of a busy day spent ministering to kids. You feel tired and drained, but because you were faithful you know God smiled on your efforts.

Today God smiled when...

If God can speak through a burning bush, a donkey, and—if need be—make the rocks cry out, surely he'll use a children's ministry worker who's on his or her knees. Take heart. God's ready and willing to use you!

▼ Application

Draw a heart.

Inside it, paraphrase the words of 1 Samuel 16:7b. As you meditate on what matters most to God, create a list of "Great Expectations." Write around the edges of the heart the inner qualities God calls "great" and the attitudes of the heart he "expects" to find in those who serve him. Circle the ones that you'll work on this week.

It's the Little Things That Count

"Practice hospitality" (Romans 12:13b).

- What is your definition of *hospitality*?

- How can you practice hospitality in your ministry?

▼ Training Session

Imagine going to work in the following situation.

No one greets you when you arrive. In fact, no one seems to even know your name. The chair they tell you to sit in is too small. The walls are empty and drab. The air is a little too chilly or quite muggy. You're told to write your name on a paper, but the pencil has no point. You don't understand all the directions, but by now you're too intimidated to ask questions. You wish you could just disappear.

Sounds awful, doesn't it? Would you ever want to go back to such a place? Probably not.

So why would a child want to go back to Sunday school?

The good news is that most Sunday school classrooms are anything *but* unwelcoming, drab, or inadequately resourced.

But some are—so it's wise to think about your classroom from a child's perspective.

Are the walls bright and cheery? Do the games have all the pieces they need? Do balls hold air? Are markers in working order? Do pencils have points? Are chairs comfortable? These are all the little things that add up to create a big, engaging environment for kids.

If your space needs work, invite kids to help you make changes. Not only will they have some fun ideas, but they'll also feel ownership of their environment.

But maybe you don't *have* a room. Your church rents classrooms, or your home church has just a garage available. No problem!

Just ask your kids to *imagine* the perfect room. Kids are imagination experts! They won't have any trouble pretending the room is just right.

Remember: *You're* the greatest environment-maker in your classroom! Greet each child by name, smile, laugh—show kids you're happy to be their teacher. Your welcoming attitude and genuine love can make even a garage warm and welcoming.

Take this training deeper as you think over these questions:

- How inviting is your ministry space? Would you want to be there every week if you were a child?

- What steps do you need to take to make your space more inviting?

▼ Journal

Lord, help me have the eyes of a child. Help me to remember what works for kids and what doesn't. Guide me as I think about making these changes...

▼ Application

You're creative. You're fun. If you weren't, you wouldn't be teaching kids. Let some of that fun and creativity shine through as you look at ways to make your ministry space more inviting.

Pretend you're one of the kids in your class. No, *really* pretend. Get down at your kids' level to view your room. If you teach younger children, that means we want you to start in the hallway and literally crawl through your classroom to see the room as your students do. If you teach older kids, sit in a rolling chair as you observe the room from their standpoint.

What do you see? Are the pictures too high for little ones to see? Are the chairs too small for your kids? Go through every part of your room and supplies, making notes as if you were one of your own students. Then make a list of what changes you think need to be made. And remember, enlist the help of your students as you plan and dream.

Adapting to the Unexpected

 ## ▼ Training Session

"Many are the plans in a man's heart, but it is the Lord's purpose that prevails" (Proverbs 19:21).

- What will help you make plans that are pleasing to God?

- What do you think is God's overall purpose for your ministry?

If there's one thing you can count on when teaching kids, it's that you can't count on things going as planned.

We've all been there. You stayed up the night before class, carefully cutting out the foil patterns you'd need to make the angel craft the next morning. You even thought ahead and cut a few extras in case you had visitors. Pretty smart, right?

Right! But who knew that so many families would have so many out-of-town guests who would have *so many* kids? And all those extra kids somehow ended up in your class! No way do you have enough foil patterns to make that many angels! What do you do? Scrap the craft? That works, but then what do you replace it with?

Sound familiar? The solution is all about adapting. And all about not having to be perfect.

Things won't always go as planned. It's just a fact of life. So when the unexpected happens, don't beat yourself up about it. Just move on and do your best.

By the way, here are two alternatives for your foil shortage:

- You could have kids form pairs or even trios, and each group could make an angel. Then instead of each child taking an angel craft home, you could have groups display their angels in the hallway or foyer.

- Or you could quickly cut more patterns from construction or copier paper, so kids can make a variety of angels.

The key is to not panic or get caught up in blaming yourself. Instead, move ahead.

If you have more kids in class than you expected, have kids form groups during activities. Scout around and see if any classrooms have an extra volunteer to spare. Or explain the situation to your students and ask for their suggestions. Involving kids in the discussion empowers them and often results in great solutions.

The same holds true if you have too *few* kids show up. Explain the game or activity to your kids, and let them think of creative solutions. Kids may opt to play numerous roles in a play, or they may play a game as a large group rather than in teams.

Trust yourself and trust your kids. Together, you can adapt to any situation!

Take this training deeper as you think over these questions:

- How flexible are you in your teaching?
- What kinds of situations bring you to a halt in the classroom?
- How can you more easily adapt to unexpected situations as you teach?

▼ Journal

Help me to remember that I don't have to be perfect and that you'll help me in every situation. I especially need help when…

As you think about your teaching ministry, focus on your relationships. Trust your relationship with God. Foster your relationship with your students. Then when the unexpected happens, you'll have a firm rock to stand on as you survey the situation and implement your solutions.

▼ Application

Write a "Worst Case Scenario" sketch as you think of what could happen if *way* too many kids come to your next class. You might write, "I'll panic when I see that many kids. And then they'll all start making noise and running around. And then everyone in the building will know I've lost control. And then someone will discover the snack. And then…" Go ahead—put down your worst fears. Then do the same exercise as you think about having too few kids in class.

Then read over what you wrote. First, you'll see that most of what you fear is unrealistic. Most of what you wrote will never happen (and definitely not all at once). Second, you'll be able to constructively think of ways to solve the situations that may actually occur—in advance!

Time Trials

> "Guard the good deposit that was entrusted to you—guard it with the help of the Holy Spirit who lives in us" (2 Timothy 1:14).

• Why is the Holy Spirit's help invaluable when things don't go as planned?

• In your ministry role with children, how are you guarding the "deposit" of time God entrusts to you each week?

TICK TICK

▼ Training Session

Children's ministry has its own time zone.

Some weeks the time flies by. Other weeks the time drags.

Plus, you're often at the mercy of "big church," other classes, or any number of outside variables that stretch and squeeze your time. So what can you do?

To be ready for a shortened class time, prepare your lesson with a "first-things-first" approach. Some lessons suggest a certain order of activities. Don't interrupt that flow, but consider where your minutes will be best spent for maximum impact. Decide up front which activities you can cut and which are essential. Then guard the essentials well.

Prepare for those days the sermon goes long or your lesson runs short by preparing an "X-Tension Kit" to pull off the shelf when it's needed. Fill it with review games, simple crafts, favorite music, or other activities adaptable to any lesson focus.

Use extra minutes to reinforce the learning begun earlier. If God entrusts you with additional teaching moments, use them wisely.

Here are a few X-Tension Kit ideas to get you started:

• **Campfire testimonies.** Give each student a thin stick (pencils work in a pinch) and a large marshmallow (or cotton ball). As kids roast their marshmallows over an imaginary fire of small logs (rolled construction paper works well) and red tissue paper, have them share a prayer request, praise, or review a portion of the lesson they liked the most.

• **Hats.** Have a story "re-cap" by letting the kids wear a baseball cap as they take turns sharing a portion of the Bible story.

• **Zip-lock journal.** Give each student a resealable sandwich bag and an index card. Have kids write a short paragraph or draw a picture about the day's Bible lesson and how they'll live out what they learned. Keep the journals handy, and add cards as needed.

The only plan that works is one that allows for change. Be ready to be flexible.

Take this training deeper as you think over these questions:

• What elements of your lesson will you not surrender to a shortened class time?

• How can you be alerted week by week of possible schedule changes that will affect your class time?

• What could you put in an X-Tension Kit to use this week?

▼ Journal

As God stretches us, he promises to strengthen us. Hold a rubber band in your hand and ask God to help you remain flexible when unforeseen changes occur in your class time.

Lord, as you entrust me with moments of time that can impact children for eternity,

help me to. . .

The bottom line: Kids should leave your class knowing Jesus a little better whether they've been there for 15 minutes or 90. Only God can make that happen each week. Ask the Holy Spirit to empower you with the ability to make brief moments of time count for eternity.

▼ Application

You feed kids. Every week you serve up a plate of spiritual food to children. How can you give them a balanced diet—even if "mealtime" doesn't go as planned?

What do you want to make sure your kids are fed this week? Write it on the center of a paper plate. Add to the plate other elements of your lesson. Decide the size of each portion according to what's vital, what is important but not crucial, and what can be left out if necessary.

After class, evaluate whether your kids went away hungry or well fed, and then plan next week's menu accordingly.

Facing the Sea of Blank Stares

> "Then he opened their minds so they could understand the Scriptures" (Luke 24:45).

• When a child doesn't understand what you're saying, where does the misunderstanding lie?

• Why is it sometimes so hard to be understood?

HUH?

▼ Training Session

You're mid-lesson and you see it: a sea of blank stares. You've lost the kids. Now what?

First, seek to understand. Check in with your kids by asking, "Where did I lose you?" "How can I help you understand?" or "How would you explain in your own words what I just said?" Usually, kids can give you an idea of where they got lost.

For many children (and adults), concepts like faith, hope, love, perseverance, heaven, integrity, and the Holy Spirit are hard to grasp. Making abstract concepts clear and plain is challenging, and even the best teacher can stumble.

So do what Jesus did. Connect abstract principles with practical stories and tangible, everyday objects: seeds to explain faith, coins to teach trust and serving, and fish to talk about provision.

Link the abstract with the concrete. Show a real gift as you explain God's gift of eternal life. Shower your class with Silly String as you explain joy in worship.

Also, be sure the lesson and activities are age-appropriate.

First-graders simply aren't designed to learn the same ideas and points as fifth-graders are. Study the age group you teach. Know their capabilities and limitations.

One great place to start is with "Age-Level Insights" in Children's Ministry Magazine. Check out a child development book. Or simply spend more time hanging out with kids in the age group you teach.

A more challenging source of blank stares is when kids simply don't *want* to learn. They'd rather talk—or yawn—and refuse to engage with you or the lesson.

And try as you might, you can't *make* a student understand—or even want to try.

But you *can* help students find an ounce of motivation. Here are a couple ways:

• **Focus on the fun in learning.** Ask kids what would help them enjoy class time. Note their suggestions and work them into your lesson.

• **Make learning relevant.** Kids check out when there's a lack of connection between the lesson and their lives. Kids (and, again, adults) always ask the question, "So what does this have to do with me?" Answer that question up front.

Blank stares aren't the end of your lesson; they're an invitation to tweak your lesson and reconnect!

Take this training deeper as you think over these questions:

- How can you better gauge whether kids understand?

- What's the hidden curriculum kids learn when you are flexible enough to adjust your approach because of their confusion?

▼ Journal

Flexibility is patience practiced! Write down the things you do to relax, and brainstorm a way to use just one of those to diffuse your classroom frustrations. Then place your hand on each one and pray that God will bear fruit in your flexible, teachable attitude.

Some you win, some get rained out, but you have to suit up for them all!

▼ Application

Write down a list of questions you can ask yourself and your students next time you find yourself teaching to a sea of blank faces. Keep this list of questions handy as you teach. Post it on a wall, fold it into your teacher guide, or stick it in your pocket.

Sub Power: A Stealth Mission

> "Commit to the Lord whatever you do, and your plans will succeed" (Proverbs 16:3).
>
> ---
>
> • What are you willing to commit to the Lord right now?
>
> ---
>
> • How do you commit what you do to the Lord?

▼ Training Session

Whether you have a week to prepare or just a few minutes, substitute teaching is a vital ministry. If you're a substitute, you're not second string—you're a *real* teacher, an above-average hero.

When you're dispatched to teach on short notice or with kids you don't know, here are a few things to keep in mind.

1. **Setting sail.** How you begin sets the tone for the rest of the session. Arrive before the children do, and have something for them to do as soon as they walk in the door. If you're not quite prepared when the first child arrives, let kids help you get ready. Kids love to help the teacher!

2. **Full speed ahead!** Discussion times can sink subs. Long silences seem deadly, don't they? They seem to bring a strong lesson to a sudden halt. You're tempted to answer the questions yourself or avoid asking them altogether!
   - First, keep in mind that wait time is OK.
   - Keep discussions lively by asking easy, open-ended questions: "How did you feel during that activity?"
   - Let kids vote on answers: "Of these choices, what do you think will happen to Jonah when he goes to Nineveh?" As kids warm up, lead in to tougher questions.
   - Have kids form pairs and talk to partners. Pair-shares lower kids' defenses and encourage them to dig deeper.

3. **Bringing it back to port.** Amazingly, the most challenging time for a sub may be the *end* of the lesson. Running out of fuel sends subs to the bottom.
   - Take a sub survival kit with you. Fill a box with games and extra activity ideas to keep kids engaged and actively learning.

Success in subbing is connected to prayer and to focus. By staying focused on the essentials, your lesson will naturally fall into place as you go. Prepare for subbing even further by doing the following:
- Find the class list, allergy list, and emergency information.
- Visit classes before you teach to observe routines and meet the children.
- Know before class how you'll respond to sick, unruly, or timid children. This reduces stress when these problems, especially disciplinary ones, arise.
- Pray for God's gift of joy as you embark on your new adventure!

Take this training deeper as you think over these questions:

- What blessings has God given you through substitute teaching?

- How can you improve and grow as you teach each class?

▼ **Journal**

God, give me courage as I...

Lord, help me when I'm uncertain about...

What a blessing to be a substitute teacher! Not only do you get the opportunity to walk in someone else's shoes, you get to step in and change lives. God appreciates your stealth work. Although you may feel like you're sailing under the radar, your service is so very powerful. Thank you for being an unsinkable sub!

▼ Application

Bring a written goal to class along with a personal item that you can place prominently in the room as a focal point. You may choose to bring a box, Bible, paperweight, or picture. This item is for you—to remind you why you're teaching. Don't forget to wear a name tag, and proudly add the title "Sub" to it!

Creatively Created

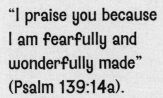

"I praise you because I am fearfully and wonderfully made" (Psalm 139:14a).

• How can you encourage individual creativity in your children?

• What specific talents do your students possess? How can you promote those talents?

▼ Training Session

You've placed a sample craft in front of your children. You've gone over all the directions—step by step—showing children how to tear cotton balls and place them in a row on the clouds, glue the green tissue paper on the bottom of the picture, and stick the cut-out flowers on top of the green tissue paper. You've done everything you can to help kids make a perfect craft.

So you can't understand why little Monica is proudly showing you her picture with the cotton balls, tissue paper, and flowers glued in a lump in the middle of the page. Wasn't she listening at *all*?

As a teacher, this is a moment where you have several options. You could tell Monica she needs to move her cotton balls and tissue paper. "Look at the sample craft," you could say, pointing out that the cut-out flowers go at the bottom with the green tissue paper. Then you could send Monica back to her table to try again.

Or you could choose to respond with love and pride when you see Monica's *unique* and *personal* craft. You could praise her for her creativity and imagination. You could ask her to explain her craft to you, and seek to understand why she mixed up the cotton balls and the green tissue paper. You might be surprised to discover that Monica loves colors all mixed together or that this is her idea of the new heaven and earth.

When you choose the second option, you're embracing creativity in your classroom. You're allowing children to express themselves and giving yourself the chance to learn more about your children. But to embrace this option, you must accept this truth: The best crafts are those that encourage creativity. Everyone's craft will look different…and that's OK.

Children don't learn through making perfect crafts. They learn through the process of creating and through debriefing the process.

Make creativity a priority in your classroom by allowing kids to use your arts and crafts time as an opportunity to express themselves and their growing friendships with God.

Take this training deeper as you think over these questions:

- What kinds of crafts allow kids to express themselves creatively? What kinds of crafts don't? (Hint: Avoid step-by-step crafts…embrace the abstract!)

- How can you help kids take ownership of their crafts?

- When are some other times in your classroom, besides arts and crafts, that you can encourage personal creativity?

▼ Journal

I feel creatively inspired when…

Have you ever just really looked at a rhinoceros? Talk about evidence of God's creativity! God is a creative God, and God created us in his image…which means God created us to be creative! Your classroom is the perfect place to encourage and inspire the God-given gift of creativity in your children!

▼ Application

Think of an object like a rose or a fish, and draw or paint it on a piece of paper. Then use the Internet to look up different artistic renditions of that object. You'll quickly find that no two artists (including you!) saw the object the same way.

Art is so amazing because it gives us so many different windows or views on the world. There would be no point in art if every artist drew a tree or a sunset in the same way. We're inspired and enriched by the arts because of the personal creativity evident in each piece.

Come to Your Senses

> "Taste and see that the Lord is good; blessed is the man who takes refuge in him" (Psalm 34:8).

- How do you "taste" the goodness of God?

- When do you see the Lord's goodness?

▼ Training Session

Ever taken a senses census? Do you ever deliberately exercise your senses to appreciate where you are and what you're doing?

We use our senses to learn, and we can utilize our students' senses as valuable classroom tools.

Take your favorite Bible story and read it carefully. See if you can detect some clues and references to what the people in the story sensed, too. Even passages that explain God's message often give some image or refer to our senses to help our understanding.

Maybe you've turned the lights on and off as you taught about Creation, or you let children hear sounds of the ocean during Jonah's story.

But have you let your students smell frankincense and myrrh? Have you had kids feel sheep's wool or cedar wood? Have you given children figs or honeycomb to taste? Have your students tried walking on palm leaves or playing a lyre?

There are many practical ways to create a sensory environment in each lesson.

Sight—To enhance lessons visually, decorate your room differently each week. For example, if the story is in a prison, use crepe paper to bar off the doors and windows. You could also show artwork based on your story or the emotions in the story.

Sound—Sound effects for stories are great, but auditory experiences can be enhanced in other ways, too. Check out some music from the library to play during your lesson. Many classical composers used specific Bible passages as inspiration for their compositions.

Taste—Need to come up with a tasty lesson? Have students create edible dough animals for Noah's ark or let your snack symbolize events in a story. For example, you could have a sweet snack, sour snack, and then another sweet snack to chronicle Job's life story. Just remember to check allergies before the lesson!

Touch and Smell—Touch and smell are easily incorporated, too. Put objects that relate to your story inside paper bags for students to feel or smell. Have students guess what's inside or how they relate to the story. Various air fresheners might help you with those hard-to-find scents to use during your class. Make scratch-and-sniff pictures with glue sticks and spices or touch-and-feel storybooks with fabric and small objects from nature.

Linking our senses to the Bible stirs emotional response and memory. We use our senses to learn and we should use this knowledge while planning our children's lessons.

Take this training deeper as you think over these questions:

- What's your favorite smell? Why is it your favorite?
- How do the senses of touch, smell, and taste come into your lesson?
- When does taking a sense away enhance the lesson?
- Why do you think God chose to link our senses so tightly with learning?

▼ Journal

God, thank you for the beauty of...

Help me to appreciate my senses when...

It's fun to look at food ads—although it usually causes cravings! If you could describe your teaching by using a famous ad slogan for food, what would it be? Remember, you are what you eat and you teach what you think. Come to your senses, and taste success in your teaching!

▼ Application

This is an assignment you'll love—you are to find a new place to eat a new food. Go to a new restaurant or coffee shop, or make a new recipe to take picnicking somewhere new.

Pay close attention to all the new things you sense and write down your sensory experiences in a journal. Add a sentence sharing how this experience can enhance your teaching—whether it is the way the meal is served, the atmosphere, the presentation, or the food itself.

Wow!

▼ Training Session

> "I tell you the truth, unless you change and become like little children, you will never enter the kingdom of heaven" (Matthew 18:3b).

• Why do you think we need to change and become like little children?

• How does your life reflect this Bible verse?

When was the last time you said, "Wow!" What are some "wow" moments in your life?

Surprise moments come in big moments—and small ones, too. The "wow" in your lesson comes from changing your students' perspectives. It comes from reminding them of Biblical truths in new and unexpected ways, just as Jesus did.

Think about how Jesus taught. He compared things that seemed unrelated, like mustard seeds and faith. He used surprise endings in his parables and sayings—no one expected the Prodigal Son to be welcomed home or the meek to inherit the earth. He also used common points of reference such as farming to illustrate how faith grows in "good soil." "Wow" moments don't have to be big, just a diversion from the expected.

Look at one of your lessons. Where's the wonder? What would a child find fascinating? How can you use something you know to teach God's Word in a way a child wouldn't know? Do you have a hobby that can help teach God's Word?

What references can you use to relate to your kids—running a race as Paul mentioned in Hebrews 12:1 or perhaps playing sports and doing homework?

If you've found experiences or objects that can add a twist, twist away! For example, if you love kaleidoscopes, give students a chance to look at one while they explore the account of Creation.

Jesus calls us to become like children—wondering like children. If we can wonder like a child, we'll be able to reach and teach children. Here are some practical ways to become childlike and add "wow" to your lesson:

▶ Go to a toy store and find the most unusual items available for your age group, then speculate what Bible story or truth the object could illustrate.

▶ Read the most popular children's stories and watch kids' movies. Think about how they can help you tell Bible stories. Perhaps you could discuss Joseph's "Series of Unfortunate Events," try Joseph's brothers on "The People's Court," or act out the Cinderella tale to compare Jacob and Esau.

▶ Invite some people the kids admire to share a Bible story or share their faith.

▶ Give a real party during Pentecost or have your class act out the good Samaritan in a real-life mission project, making "wows" by doing the unexpected.

Take this training deeper as you think over these questions:

- What "wow" activities can you list now that you might be able to use in future lessons?

- Who can serve as a resource to help you come up with "wow" ideas?

▶ **Journal**

God, give me the ability to see wonder as I . . .

Father, help me "wow" children so that they learn . . .

What a privilege to share the wonder of God's creation with children! You are a blessing and will be blessed for your efforts to show children the "wow" in God's world.

▼ Application

What makes you say, "Wow"? Imagine you're one of your students. What activities would excite you? How can you apply your excitement to your class?

Become a student, taking a class or studying something you know little about so that you can relate to what it feels like to learn something new. Write down the ways your teacher brings "wow" experiences to the classroom. Evaluate your new knowledge from this class and from the teaching methods used to see how it can inspire new "wows" in your class, too.

Everyone's Included!

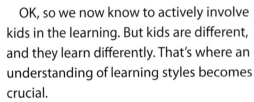

▼ Training Session

Kids (and adults!) learn by doing. It's that simple. That's why it's so important to include every child in your class in doing hands-on activities.

But not all lessons that *say* they include active learning actually do. For example, a teacher may do a perfectly acceptable object lesson in front of the class. And that's active—for the teacher, at least. But *kids* are not actively involved.

How much more effective would that object lesson be if students formed pairs and performed it themselves? And then went home and performed it with their families and friends? By having kids *do* the activity, rather than simply watch the activity, you will have exponentially increased the retention value for kids.

OK, so we now know to actively involve kids in the learning. But kids are different, and they learn differently. That's where an understanding of learning styles becomes crucial.

You could actively involve kids every week in dramas. But you probably have some kids in class who are musical learners, and some who are visual learners, and some who are kinesthetic learners. And those kids won't learn best by doing dramas every week. That's why it's important to vary the kinds of activities you do so no child will be left out of a lesson.

It's also important to make sure lessons don't include activities that inadvertently result in children being left out. Sometimes such activities are hard to spot. For example, you might play a game where only certain kids get to participate, or a game where "losers" are knocked out of the game early on. Because such games are common in secular settings, you might be tempted to overlook the fact that some kids are not actively involved throughout the game.

But if they're not involved in the play, they won't be involved in the learning. And that's your goal—to make sure that every child is involved in every activity, because that's how learning takes place!

> "Therefore encourage one another and build each other up, just as in fact you are doing" (1 Thessalonians 5:11).

• How does encouragement change your outlook?

• How can you build others up in the same ways you like to be encouraged?

Take this training deeper as you think over these questions:

- How sure are you that all of your students always participate in class? How can you make sure?

- How can you add more variety to your lessons to make sure you reach and include everyone in the lesson?

▼ Journal

I want to include each student in class in each lesson I teach. I can do that better by...

Think of it—you only get one hour each week to reach your students for God. One hour. How will you use that hour to reach each and every student? God has put the children in your class there for a reason. Make the most of the time you have together!

▼ Application

Use a marker to go through a lesson you've already taught. Next to each activity, note whether every child is actively included. At the end of the lesson, evaluate the lesson for effectiveness. Was it truly active?

Now use the same process to evaluate the next lesson you're planning to teach. Where is it weak? What can you do to make sure that every child participates in every activity? Make sure that no child is left out of the learning!

Show and Tell

▼ Training Session

Think about the most important life lesson you learned.

Now think about how you learned it. Did you read it? Probably not. Maybe you picked it up from a sermon. Doubtful. No, you're probably remembering an *experience* that led you to this important life lesson.

That's because most of us learn through experience! In fact, on average people only retain 5 to 10 percent of what they hear or read, 25 percent of what they learn through media, 40 to 60 percent of what they learn during a role-playing exercise, and 80 to 90 percent of what they experience personally and directly. Those are pretty significant percentages! And they're percentages that directly relate to our classrooms.

If our children are only retaining a small fraction (one-tenth at best!) of what they read or hear, we have to think of ways to help kids creatively *experience* learning—so they have positive and meaningful memories associated with that lesson.

Experiences are the glue of our memory because they evoke emotions. We remember more when our emotions are engaged. Emotions make learning stick in a way that everyday logic never can. As teachers, we must not ignore that fact.

So how do you create these emotion-evoking experiences in your classroom? It's simple!

Read through the next Bible story you'll be teaching and make a list of the emotions that story involves. For example, if your story is about Jesus washing his disciples' feet, the emotions involved in that story might be love, humility, vulnerability, embarrassment, and joy.

Once you have a list of emotions, think of some activities that are designed to evoke those emotions. For example, you might have kids wash a partner's feet so they can experience the vulnerability the disciples might have felt. Or you might have kids do something really gross and dirty, like taking out all the trash for the church, so they can experience the humility Jesus expressed when he served his disciples.

You're not done yet! An experience is simply an experience until you debrief it. Design two or three questions that you can ask kids after they've gone through each experience. These questions are most effective when they relate directly to kids' lives and move the experience out of the hypothetical and into the applicable. For example, you might ask kids how they felt being served and how they can serve others as Jesus served his disciples.

So now you're ready! Go out there and *experience* the difference!

"Now that I, your Lord and Teacher, have washed your feet, you also should wash one another's feet. I have set you an example that you should do as I have done for you" (John 13:14-15).

• Jesus didn't just tell his disciples to be servants, he showed them how—he used an experience. How do you think the disciples felt after having their feet washed?

• How long do you think the disciples remembered the experience of having their feet washed?

• How do you think that experience affected their lives?

Take this training deeper as you think over these questions:

- What's an experience you remember?
- What are some emotions connected with that experience?
- What Bible story evokes those same emotions?
- How could you pull those emotions into a classroom while teaching that Bible story?

▼ Journal

The most powerful experience I've ever had was when...

God, I want to follow Jesus' example as a teacher. I want to effectively use experiences and emotions to help children grow in their friendships with you. Please inspire me, encourage me, and aid me as I work to incorporate creative experiences into my classroom. In Jesus name, amen.

▼ Application

Think of a Bible story.

Now think of two or three emotions that story evokes, such as joy, frustration, fear, or hope. Imagine you're going to teach that story in your class this week.

Think of an activity for each of the emotions you listed. For example, you might come up with a game that is specifically designed to evoke the emotion of fear. Or you might design a craft that leads kids to feel joy. Come up with a full lesson plan that effectively uses each emotion in your list.

And don't forget to include debriefing questions for each activity!

Communicating Effectively With Children

▼ Training Session

Communication that's effective is characterized by shared meaning, mutually satisfying understanding, confident interactions, and results that are palpably positive. You communicate with your words, but with many other tools as well.

Effective communication is physically inviting and warm. Make non-threatening eye contact.

Smile. A lot.

Position yourself at a child's level. This lowers defenses considerably and paints a picture of openness and caring for a child.

Make sure your gestures are deliberate and full of life and warmth.

Effective communication is about sharing. This doesn't mean sharing with students what you want to say. That's preaching. It's about sharing feelings and responding to the feelings of your children. And it's about sharing the microphone.

Deliberately pause to listen to a child. This is the best way to show respect for a child's feelings. When you let children talk, you're communicating that you really, truly care for their feelings.

When children are hurting, share their feelings.

Rejoice with kids who are happy and excited. By sharing with them in their time of joy, you're communicating more effectively than you ever would with plain words.

Effective communication is measured. Are you aware of how children perceive you? Continually do a self-check to see how you're coming across to kids.

Watch body language. If kids are pulling back, maybe your communication is a little harsh. If they're constantly straining to hear or understand you, perhaps you need to be more clear.

Check the balance of communication. Are you allowing kids to give you honest feedback? Do you let them have a turn to talk and ask questions?

Measuring your communication is a lot like looking in the mirror. Check your focus often.

Effective communication involves laughter and delight. Kids are drawn to those who make them feel great. If you want to engage children, play with them!

Laugh with kids (at the appropriate times).

Involve yourself in their activities. As you participate enthusiastically with kids doing things they enjoy, you'll deepen your connection with them and open more doors for greater communication. Participate in everything with a sense of delight and enjoyment.

And by all means smile!

"I no longer call you servants, because a servant does not know his master's business. Instead, I have called you friends, for everything that I learned from my Father I have made known to you" (John 15:15).

• How do you think it felt to be called Jesus' friend?

• How are you a friend to the children in your class?

Take this training deeper as you think over these questions:

• Rate yourself on the four facets of communication on the other side of this page. Where do you need to improve?

• Is your classroom a laboratory of discovery where conversation is give and take?

• How do you feel when people preach at you? Listen to you?

• When is it hard to smile with children? How can you overcome that?

▶ Journal

Describe the last class you actually had fun in and smiled a lot.
What were the key ingredients that made it fun?

Children rarely remember what you say. They rarely remember what you do. But they'll never forget the way you make them feel!

▼ Application

Take turns talking to your spouse or friend by having that person sit while you stand. Then reverse the positions so your spouse or friend is standing while you're sitting.

How did it feel to be the "short" person? Why?

How did it feel to "talk down" to your spouse or friend? Why?

Welcome!

> "Jesus said, 'Let the little children come to me, and do not hinder them, for the kingdom of heaven belongs to such as these' " (Matthew 19:14).

• What does it mean to have childlike faith?

• Jesus genuinely cared about children; how can you show that same caring in your ministry?

▼ Training Session

Jesus welcomed children and wanted relationships with them. Though he was surrounded on all sides by throngs of people, Jesus nurtured the children in his midst. We'd do well to follow his example.

Take the initiative to get to know the children in your class. Here are a few easy tips to help you get started:

- **Talk eye to eye.** If you're teaching younger children, squat down so you can make direct eye contact.

- **Greet kids by name.** Let your students know that you're glad they're in class!

- **Show kids you value them by being in class on time and having quality supplies ready.** Periodically go through your supply closet to make sure crayons and pencils are sharpened and game balls are inflated.

- **Find out what sports your students play and what their favorite (or least favorite) school subjects are.** Jot notes so you can remember to ask the next week how the soccer game went. You could even go to the soccer game!

- **Offer to pray for your students—then pray!** Follow up the next week on whatever the prayer request was. Let kids know that you've been praying for them.

- **Engage kids in meaningful conversation, using open-ended questions rather than questions that require a "yes" or "no" answer.** For example, you'll learn far more by asking, "When is a time you had to forgive someone?" than by asking "Have you ever forgiven someone?" Kids know you're interested in them and their answers when you ask open-ended questions.

And nothing communicates care like listening when kids talk.

Make your kids feel cherished. Most adults don't make the effort to truly see children. Be the exception to the rule and you'll quickly become a favorite grown-up!

Take this training deeper as you think over these questions:

- How welcome do the kids in your class really feel? How do you know?

- What can you do better to show your students that you value them?

- How well do you really listen to your students? How can you listen better?

▼ Journal

*Lord, please give me the energy and imagination to truly welcome children to my class.
Help me to follow your example by...*

You have the awesome opportunity to welcome children into the kingdom of God. Be assured that the little things you do and say in class can have an eternal impact. Rely on Jesus to help you welcome your students, just as he did.

▼ Application

Try this little self-awareness test. For each person in class, make a list of what you know about that child—likes and dislikes, sports, musical instruments, siblings, and special needs.

Then decide what you can do to foster a deeper relationship with each student. Commit to one simple idea to make each child feel more valued and welcomed in class. For example, you might simply ask a student how basketball is going or write a child a brief note of appreciation. Whatever you do, you'll be making a positive impact on that child's life!

Are We Having Fun Yet?

> "A cheerful heart is good medicine, but a crushed spirit dries up the bones" (Proverbs 17:22).

- When do you have the most fun working with children?

- Would you describe yourself as a cheerful and fun person? Why or why not?

▼ Training Session

As a dedicated children's worker, you connect with kids week after week. Your path crosses theirs at Sunday school, children's church, midweek programs, or any number of other ministry events.

You're spending time with kids, but are you having *fun* with them?

Is your teaching time filled with warmth, delight, and fun?

God's Word is serious stuff—but that doesn't mean it should be stuffy.

A classroom where kids are learning is usually loud and punctuated by laughter. Fun opens the doors to relationships—and the best, longest-lasting learning takes place in the context of relationships.

Learn what your kids' definition of fun is—what tickles their funny bones and makes them laugh. Then work that into your teaching. As long as it's not from put-down humor, laughter is welcome.

Kids need to sense your genuine enjoyment of them; it's how they know they're loved. So step into their world, and start giggling. When you open God's Word to teach, you'll find that a happy audience is a receptive audience.

And do this to keep things fun: dull-proof your Bible lessons. Try new ideas frequently. Pull out the stops with something outrageously new. For instance:

- Learn to speak a dialect and be your own guest speaker as you present your lesson using an accent. Take it up a notch and interview yourself.

- Ask to borrow some beach chairs and blankets, line them up in the grass, and take your kids out of the classroom and to the beach.

- Share prayer requests by borrowing some cell phones so kids can call one another—then put the phones away and call on the Lord together.

Ten years from now it won't be what was written on a workbook page that your kids remember. It will be YOU—the teacher they knew as a fun friend.

Take this training deeper as you think over these questions:

- How do your kids define fun? What makes them laugh?

- How much healthy laughter can be heard outside the door of your classroom?

- How can you have fun with your students but still retain an atmosphere of order and respect?

Journal

Lord, in your presence is a fullness of joy. As I spend time with my students this week, let my presence with them reflect your joy by...

It's easy to drag the weight of the world with us into our classrooms. When that happens, kids don't see "burdened" adults. They see grumpy people who are no fun. Leave your finances, migraine, and hectic schedule at the Cross—and at the classroom door. The joy of the Lord is your strength. Use it.

▼ Application

Contemplate a recent event in your classroom that was anything but fun. Perhaps it was an annoying interruption or a lesson that went south. How could the use of humor and a fun-loving nature have helped turn things around?

Create a "before" and "after" comic strip. The first part depicts what actually happened; the second part shows how humor could have lightened the situation.

Time Well Spent

▼ Training Session

"I always thank my God as I remember you in my prayers, because I hear about your faith in the Lord Jesus and your love for all the saints" (Philemon 1:4-5).

• How can praying for and spending time with students build a firmer foundation for their lives?

• How can we inspire faith in students by forming relationships with them?

Think about your closest friends. How did you become close? Probably not by simply spending a short time together, making your friends call you by your last name.

Most friendships are developed through quality time spent together. Lots of quality time!

Over cups of coffee on rainy days. Getting together for dessert and games on weekends. Discussing the Big Life Questions together.

Your kids deserve the same.

You probably can't spend the same amount of time with each child in your class as you do with your closest friends, but you can find *some* time to get to know kids personally—and to let them get to know you.

Remember: It's OK to interrupt a lesson to spend time on relationships. Try these ideas:

• **Spend one-on-one time in class.** If class size and volunteer numbers permit, take a few minutes out of each lesson to spend time with each child. Ask questions. Really listen to the answers. Find out what life is like for each student.

• **Stop to play.** Children love to play. They love to imagine. So do that. Bring in a game. Write a story together. Fire up your imagination!

• **Work *with* them.** We teachers often direct kids to do a project and then coach them through it. Instead, do the project *with* them. When kids are working in groups, join a group and take part. If kids are working alone, do the same project alone as well.

Don't limit your time spent with kids to just time in the classroom, though. There are numerous things you can do with kids outside of class—safely:

• **Attend their events.** Learn what kinds of sports and extracurricular activities your students are involved in. Then make it a point to attend one for each child.

• **Have a party at your house.** Invite your whole class over. You can make the food, or have kids bring something.

• **Spend one-on-one time outside of class.** Kids love one-on-one attention. Be careful, though. Know your church's policy for safety. Consult parents to ask for written permission. Hang out with students in public places. You may even want to make this a two-on-one time so you have witnesses.

The more children experience healthy relationships at church, the more likely they are to have a healthy relationship with Jesus.

Take this training deeper as you think over these questions:

- In number of minutes, how much time do you intentionally spend getting to know children in your class?

- Would your students say the same?

- How can you safely spend time with kids outside of class?

▼ Journal

I can better connect to students by...

God has blessed you with a role in the lives of several children in your church. It's an exciting thing and the more you embrace the idea of truly knowing and caring for your students, the more you will be a Christ-like presence and example in their lives. It's a high calling, one that you are investing eternal treasure in.

▼ Application

With your students in mind, consider what it means to be a shepherd and friend in their lives. Plan something fun and unexpected to show them you thought about them during the week. For example, bring a special treat, make them each a special card, pay a house visit this week. Tell them how much you enjoy spending time with them each week.

Open-Door Policy

> "And do not forget to do good and to share with others, for with such sacrifices God is pleased" (Hebrews 13:16).

• How do you share your life with your students?

• Does this verse apply to your current methods of teaching? If not, how can you put this verse into action?

▼ Training Session

Remember seeing one of your teachers in the grocery store when you were a child? You may have been shocked. Teachers eat? They have a life outside of school?

The teachers who were distant or mysterious you've probably forgotten. You remember the ones who had a relationship with you and gave you a glimpse into their lives. They were real!

Squeeze into the shoes of a child for a moment. What are some of the things children wonder about their teachers?

What time does she go to bed?

What's his favorite food?

What makes her scared? happy? frustrated?

What does his house look like?

How does she spend her time when she's not at church?

Kids love to know the nitty-gritty, quirky details of the people they meet. It's a way for them to connect.

Open the door into your life. Let kids see who you are.

• Perhaps you could tell your students what life was like when you were growing up and how you noticed God working in your everyday life.

• Listen to children's stories and experiences, and tell kids about similar situations in your life.

• Tell children your favorite color, food, movie, music, hobby, or a funny story from your childhood.

• Talk about where you work and a highlight from your week.

• Share your goals and dreams.

• Tell kids what God's doing in your life and what you've been praying about lately.

God has revealed himself to us through his Word and through Christ. God wants us to know him. For us to have a relationship with God, we *have* to know him. Your kids need to know you, too. When they do, you'll help create a safe, loving, and more relaxed environment for your students. And you'll encourage kids to grow closer to the creator of relationships!

Take this training deeper as you think over these questions:

- What do you know about your students' lives? Do they currently know as much about your life?

- What are some specific stories you could share with your class about
  - ⊠ your childhood?
  - ⊠ how Jesus was revealed to you?
  - ⊠ struggles you have now or had when you were a child?

- What can you share with your students about your faith?

▼ **Journal**

Lord, humble me to be comfortable to share my life with my students and give me strength to be open and honest with them as I . . .

Lord, bless me with some ideas of how I can share my life with my students, particularly . . .

There's no higher calling than that of sharing Christ with another, especially when the *another* is a child!

▼ Application

Do you remember how exciting Show and Tell was when you were a child? Play a little Show and Tell in your classroom.

Bring in some photos of your childhood family and show them to your class. As you share your pictures, talk about them and tell some stories about them. Also, tell kids about how and when you became a Christian. Share with them how Jesus has changed your life.

You're in the Family Business, Too!

"These commandments that I give you today are to be upon your hearts. Impress them on your children. Talk about them when you sit at home and when you walk along the road, when you lie down and when you get up" (Deuteronomy 6:6-7).

• What is the church's role in helping families strengthen their faith?

• How can talking and praying with families build relationships that help them grow closer to God?

▼ Training Session

It's no secret that many families are sinking. And they're reaching for help—for someone to throw the life preserver.

When working with your kids, don't forget their families.

Church must be a place where families are valued, where they can seek refuge from the raging waters they're struggling to float in. That's where we, as the teachers of their children, come in.

What do you know about your students' families and home lives? Have you at least met the parents of all your students?

Start with that. Families need to know that you're approachable and excited to have a role in their lives.

Initiate contact. Phone parents to thank them for the contributions their kids make in class. Be specific; parents will be grateful you take a personal interest in their children.

After you make initial contact, ask questions that will give you insight into their home life: What do you like to do as a family? When do you spend the most time together? What are some issues that you're working through with your children? How can I help?

As you continue building relationships with families, encourage them in their spiritual growth. Give parents resources that strengthen their faith together. Here are a few ideas to get you started:

- Provide a half-dozen ideas for family devotions. The curriculum you use probably has a devotion option. Share it with families.

- Mail monthly "fridge fliers" with themes, special projects, memory verses, and questions to prompt spiritual discussions.

- Create drive-home discussion questions to open up dialogue about what children learned at church.

Some families might politely decline your invitation to build a relationship. Without invading their privacy, be persistent. It's important that you work on that relationship. Explain that their children will benefit from such a connection. Your friendship and willingness to work together will help each child feel important and loved—and make the classroom more relevant.

When you build relationships with families, you help those families plant their kids on an unshakable foundation.

Take this training deeper as you think over these questions:

- Why is family ministry so important in this field?

- How do children benefit when we focus on families?

- What steps can you take to create a bridge for children between church and home?

▶ Journal

Lord, help me to be open to moments where I can connect with the families whose children I teach. Help me to find time to...

God has created us for relationship. He has set us up to be his family. When you reach out to the families in your church, you're extending God's family.

▼ Application

Write a card to mail to three families you want to encourage and connect with. Point out the unique, positive qualities you see in their children, and tell them how much you look forward to getting to know them better.

Choose three families each week. Find some time in your schedule to write a card to each family so you're making connections with every family.

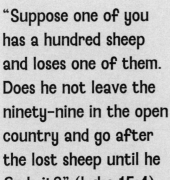
Lost Lambs

> "Suppose one of you has a hundred sheep and loses one of them. Does he not leave the ninety-nine in the open country and go after the lost sheep until he finds it?" (Luke 15:4).

- Are you willing to leave your flock in order to reach out to one lost lamb?

- What's it like to introduce a child to Jesus for the first time?

▼ Training Session

Teaching *about* Jesus is important. But leading children to a relationship with Jesus makes your teaching eternally important!

You're in the life-changing business. So are you changing lives? Are you reaching out to kids who don't *know* Jesus? As a life-changer, that's part of your mission: to reach out to lost children and change their lives. Jesus' ministry was marked by compassion: He went after the lost with love and an invitation to follow him.

Everything you teach—and each relationship you build—must have a compassion focus. What does compassion look like in your ministry?

Is it lavishly loving every child who walks in your door?

Is it plain tolerance, saying, "I'm just glad these kids are here," then thinking, *Now get off the ceiling fan and quit jamming paper in your ears*?

Is it an action—doing everything in your power to reach every child—or is it an emotion—sensing the need of lost children?

The good news: Compassion can be any and all of these. Simply put, it's loving the lost.

No doubt you're compassionate about children. What teacher isn't? But translating that compassion into action can become a sticking point for many teachers. Here are some tips for weaving compassion into your classroom.

- **Accept everyone.** When a child enters your room in tattered, faded clothes, clearly in need of a shower, do you back away? Or do you put your arm around the child, saying, "I'm so glad you're here!"—and mean it? Send the message that you *are* glad they're here.

- **Strive to meet all needs.** This opens up a welcome environment for everyone. Ask kids what they need from you. They're usually able to tell you. Also ask parents what *they* believe their kids need. Then take steps—one at a time—to meet those needs. You'll send a message of compassion quickly.

- **Meet kids where they're at.** Your kids fall along a spectrum: Some are being raised in Christian homes, others are experiencing their first day in a church. All of them are on a journey. And they need you to walk with them—wherever they are.

- **Model Christ.** Show kids what it means to live in relationship with Jesus. This sends the strongest message of all.

Compassion is the first step in changing lives. We can't *make* kids have a relationship with Jesus. But we *can* motivate them to want one!

Love the lambs.

Take this training deeper as you think over these questions:

- How do you know when a child has a friendship with Jesus?

- Do you know which children in your class now might not *know* Jesus?

- How do you currently show compassion in your classroom? What's another step you can take?

▼ Journal

*The feeling of compassion results from your thoughts about your own emotions!
How does it make you feel when you think
one of your students might not know Jesus personally?*

Thank you for your compassion for children. Thank you for walking with them on their journey. May God guide you as you partner with children in faith.

▼ Application

This week do something new to show each child who walks through your door an act of love. If you've never given children a few moments of individual attention, give that a try. If you don't usually tell kids how glad you are they're here, say it. You could even give each child a personalized welcome card.

Practice compassion for everyone. Physically meeting kids at the door will send a message that you're excited to spiritually meet and walk with them.

Sharing Your Faith Story

▼ Training Session

> "But in your hearts set apart Christ as Lord. Always be prepared to give an answer to everyone who asks you to give the reason for the hope that you have. But do this with gentleness and respect" (1 Peter 3:15).

- How prepared are you to share your faith story with your students?

- How would you present your testimony to a lively group of kids and live to tell about it?

The Scouts claim the motto "Be prepared." But God thought of it first. He asks that we always be ready to share our faith. That means with a kid-size audience, too.

Your students need to know the reason for the hope you have. Show them how you've grown in your relationship with Jesus. It's a great idea to share your faith story with your kids.

Children are a unique audience. So telling your story in a child-friendly way requires some unique preparation.

Kids need to know you've been where they are. Granted, you've lived before iPods, cell phones, and possibly even color TVs (an ancient invention, according to children). But every adult shares some measure of common ground with kids.

Did you hate math?

Did you feed your broccoli to the dog and lie to your mom about eating it?

Did your grandpa teach you how to fish?

Building your faith story around familiar experiences connects shared territory. Plus, kids can see that you've been where they are. You can help kids tie *their* present with *your* past. Just use an object from your childhood: a baseball glove, a doll, or a trophy. Let kids touch it, feel it, as you tell your faith story.

Express your story with more than mere words. Use objects that appeal to the senses to capture kids' attention—and to open the door of their understanding.

Once it's open, make sure the message is clear. The need for a relationship with Christ and how to grow closer to him are "gotta say" elements of any faith story. They should be woven in and out of your experiences in words that are easily understood.

The undiluted message of salvation, under the conviction of the Holy Spirit, can be understood and received by any child. It's your privileged duty to make the Gospel message clear. God will draw to himself those who hear the good news and receive it.

Take this training deeper as you think over these questions:

- What common ground from your childhood do you share with the kids you teach?

- In what unique, off-the-wall way can your faith story be seen and heard? eaten? touched? smelled?

- What are four "gotta say" points that you must not leave out of your faith story so kids can see what a growing relationship with Jesus is like?

▼ **Journal**

My faith story is unique. I came to faith in Christ...

You have a salvation story that can be shared in any number of ways. Ask God to help you develop a pint-size faith story, then let him empower you to share it. By God's grace, your story will plant the seeds of salvation in the heart of a child.

▼ Application

Recount a major childhood memory that your kids will relate to. Build your faith story around that experience. Imagine that you have only five to seven minutes in which to share the plan of salvation with a 10-year-old. Try to use each of the five senses. How would you creatively share your faith story, keeping the message of salvation clear?

When Is a Child Ready?

> "In him we were also chosen, having been predestined according to the plan of him who works out everything in conformity with the purpose of his will" (Ephesians 1:11).

- What does this verse say about a person's readiness to make a faith decision?

- Based on this verse, how can you know a child's ready?

▼ Training Session

You've probably noticed that kids grow, physically and spiritually, at different rates. The timing varies.

Some children are ready to make a faith decision quite early. For others it takes a major life change or experience. And still others don't want to make a decision at all—or they wait till the teenage or adult years!

Of course, deciding *not* to make a faith decision is making a decision.

Look back at Ephesians 1:11. Essentially it's up to God. Case closed.

But take heart! You have a powerful hand in it, too. God's using you to help children make that decision. Though you have little to do with *when* children choose to follow Jesus, God puts you in their lives for when children *do* make that choice.

So relax. God will make it clear to you.

For now, be prepared. The important thing is that you're ready when the child's ready.

Sometimes kids make it obvious when they're ready: "I'm not a Christian, and I want to be" or "I want to be Jesus' friend."

Sometimes they hint: "How do you know if you're going to heaven or not?" or "I don't think I'm good enough to be a Christian."

When you hear these statements, stop and make sure kids understand. Ask, "Do you realize that God wants you as a friend—and that will forever change your life?" If you know they're ready, talk more about it in private.

Many times, though, kids don't make it as obvious: A child interrupts your lesson on Noah's ark, "Why did God close the door on all those drowning people?"

Gulp! You realize your answer could help the child decide to follow that same God who shut the door—or it could turn him away.

When children bring up questions or statements like those, pause and ask God for guidance. Respond gently with probing questions. You may find that the child was just curious about the ark. Kids are always searching. They just need more help in getting there. Be patient.

The moment that a child's ready depends on the child—and on God's work. How we respond when a child *is* ready is critical. Talk with the child in private about the decision and what it means. Then encourage the child to talk to Jesus about it, asking Jesus to forgive him or her and be a forever friend. And make sure you let the parents in on the spiritual growth!

What an honor to impact a child in this way!

Take this training deeper as you think over these questions:

- Why is a private talk with a child more beneficial to determine the right time for a faith decision?

- What are some other not-so-obvious statements you've heard that indicate a child's readiness to commit to Jesus?

- When a conversation in public makes for the right time to explain the plan of salvation, will you know what to say?

▼ Journal

God, I want to help kids know you. Show me. . .

Following Jesus is an individual decision, but it's also a great group activity! Families who are following Christ together warmly share in the struggles and triumphs that accompany this fulfilling relationship. You are also important to share just how a Christian ought to live! Smile, they're watching you!

▼ Application

Look over the next few weeks' lessons. There's probably one ideal story, or section, that leads into a frank talk about a child's faith commitment. In the weeks leading up to this lesson, pray specifically about what you'll say—and for those specific children you feel are not aware of Christ's desire to be their forever friend!

Celebrate With Angels

> "In the same way, I tell you, there is rejoicing in the presence of the angels of God over one sinner who repents" (Luke 15:10).

• How often do you celebrate with new Christians?

• How can you rejoice like the angels of God when a child makes a decision to have a relationship with Jesus?

▼ Training Session

Each year we celebrate many special occasions: birthdays, holidays, new seasons, milestones. So why not celebrate the most important thing in a child's life—a decision to follow Jesus? It's a birthday, holiday, new season, and milestone—all in one! It's a time when God's angels rejoice over spiritual birth.

Let's rejoice with them.

• Give new Christians an opportunity to share their faith stories with other kids. Kids who love the spotlight will be happy to share. Those who don't may want to write their stories down.

• Give kids memorable, personalized gifts. Make a plaque. Personalize a Bible. Whatever you choose, make it special.

• Invite the class to pray with the new Christian. Pray for a growing faith and love for Jesus.

• Put an announcement in the church bulletin or newsletter.

• Give each new Christian a prayer journal. Write a special prayer or note on the first page.

• Kids always love parties. Let them help you decorate. Throw on some praise music. Play a fun game.

Always be prepared for a celebration. Since kids make faith decisions on God's time, it could happen at any moment!

Like to give something to kids when they become Christians? Have some gifts ready to personalize and present as soon as a child makes the decision.

Want to throw a party? Set some streamers and balloons nearby, ready to be put up on a moment's notice.

When a child decides to follow Jesus, don't stop at just a one-time celebration. It's an ongoing journey. Be a trusted guide. Make sure the child knows you're available to help him or her grow.

You're in a special place. Celebrate with the angels.

Take this training deeper as you think over these questions:

- Why do you think it's important to make a big deal when a child makes a faith decision to follow Christ?

- How do faith celebrations affect your children?

- What action will you take to be like the angels by rejoicing when a child makes a decision to follow Christ?

▼ Journal

I'm praying specifically for these kids to make a commitment to Christ...

Lord, I celebrate when...

Lord, you know the heart of every child in my classroom. Bless me with opportunities to celebrate. I desire to make a big deal of children's faith decisions. Give me wisdom as I lead my children in their faith journeys. In Jesus' name, amen.

▼ Application

Birthday parties take time to plan. Be ready for the appearance of that all-important surprise spiritual birthday party by preparing ahead of time. Keep all your party supplies handy and ready to go.

Whatever the plan for your celebration, being prepared will help things run smoothly—and will allow you to focus on rejoicing with the angels during the party!

Pet Peeves

"In all my prayers for all of you, I always pray with joy because of your partnership in the gospel from the first day until now, being confident of this, that he who began a good work in you will carry it on to completion until the day of Christ Jesus" (Philippians 1:4-6).

• How can you partner with kids?

• How can you stay focused on the fact that kids are growing?

▼ Training Session

We all have pet peeves. And teachers have them in the classroom. What's yours?

Gum smacking? Uncontrolled wiggling? Incessant tapping?

Not all pet peeves require our attention. Some may be distracting to kids. Others are just plain annoying—to you. Decide which is which.

There's a fine line between when to write an action off as your own pet peeve and when it needs your attention. If you're the only one in the room who seems to notice, you can probably write it off. If it's distracting others, call attention to it.

Keep in mind: Calling attention to an action can heighten the distraction—and take away from the lesson. Weigh your options. If you tell a child to stop twirling his shoelaces and pay attention, will it benefit the whole class? Or will it simply cause everyone else to look at his shoelaces? Most likely if you take the time to point it out, it's a bigger deal than it ever was before. Just let it go.

Maybe you notice a girl staring at a fly on the wall during your discussion. Is she paying attention to the fly or to the discussion? Asking her will probably make everyone else notice the fly. Instead, ask the girl a direct question related to the discussion. Then no one else will notice the fly, and you'll know if she's on the same page as you.

If someone's tapping on the table, check to see if other students are distracted. If so, whisper a request to that child, "Can you try tapping on your legs, instead?" If no one seems to notice the behavior, don't turn it into a problem.

Let's do an about-face now. While teachers have pet peeves, so do kids. It's hard to admit, but we do things kids don't like, too. Some kids just don't respond well to certain personalities.

If a child checks out during a specific time in your lesson, inventory your own behaviors. What's causing that child to lose focus? Maybe you're doing something he or she doesn't like.

Or maybe some children react negatively when you say something to them individually. Talk to those kids—find out what you said. Then say it differently next time.

Many behavior problems can be chalked up to simple annoyances. Work on discerning between pet peeves and willful defiance. When you do, you'll find ways to connect with every student.

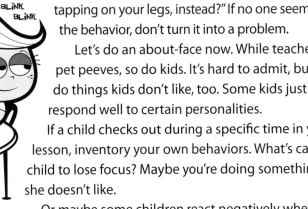

77

Take this training deeper as you think over these questions:

- How do you handle annoying behavior? What can you do better?
- What's the difference between annoyances and willful defiance?
- What kinds of questions can you ask yourself in the moment to help you discern between a pet peeve and a distraction?

▶ Journal

Lord, give me insight as I love the kids of my class...

You're the one they'll remember for years to come. May they remember you for the time, love, warmth, and attention you gave to them...even when they were hard to teach. You're investing in lives. Invest wisely.

▼ Application

Next time you teach, write down each behavior that annoys you. After you've presented your lesson, look over the list. Which behaviors can be written off as pet peeves and ignored? Which need to be addressed?

~~Noisy~~ *ACTIVE* Learning

"Shout for joy to the Lord, all the earth" (Psalm 100:1).

• How does a shout for joy sound?

• Have you ever let children shout to the Lord?

• How is this like or unlike what happens in a classroom of active children?

▼ Training Session

Do you get anxious with a noisy classroom? Maybe you're worried parents and other adults will think of your kids as rambunctious. Or as kids get louder, you're afraid they'll progress into an out-of-control army.

There's good news: Noisy learning can actually be *active* learning! Think of it as noise with a purpose.

There are four traits of active learning that can lead to a noisy (in a good way) classroom.

- **Active learning involves everyone.** Each child experiences the activity. Everyone has a part in the drama. No one's left out of a game—that means no one loses. It's participatory.

- **Active learning's an adventure.** It makes children (and even teachers) wonder what'll happen next. It's that edge-of-the-seat anticipation. Sure it's risky…but that's the point! Take risks. Kids may get loud. You may not know what'll happen. But that's the beauty of it. It's not scripted.

- **Active learning evokes an emotional response.** Laughter. Anxiety. Frustration. Let your kids experience these emotions.

- **Active learning is focused through debriefing.** Pull the whole experience together. Ask open-ended questions—apply the experience to Scripture and to life.

Plug these characteristics into a formula. What do you get? Noise. This is when what seems like a lesson out of control is really a great teacher at work! Kids are engaged. They're having fun. Don't be afraid of that.

But maybe the teacher who shares a partition with you *is* afraid of that. Try these ideas so you don't turn other teachers against you in a noise war.

- Ask other classes in earshot if they mind your class being loud for about 10 minutes. Then respect that time frame.
- Hold the noisy part of your class outside or in the gym.
- Suggest to your kids that they see how long they can whisper their joy.

And about your fear of losing control: With active learning, you won't. Use a creative noisemaker to help with that. Get a train whistle. Play music as kids work, then turn it off when it's time to focus their attention somewhere else. When kids are engaged, they're focused.

Take this training deeper as you think over these questions:

- Out-of-control or active learning? Which classroom do you feel like you have?

- Why is active learning noisy?

- What will you implement in your classroom to make it a little more active?

▼ **Journal**

Lord, I want to move into active learning in my classroom. Here are my fears...

Picture your students learning right now! What does it look like? You can make that picture a permanent feature in your classroom.

▼ Application

Go to your library. Sit in a corner with your eyes closed. Just listen for five minutes. What do you learn?

Now go to a busy place—a supermarket, airport, subway station, or coffee shop. Do the same thing. What do you learn?

Where did you learn the most? Why? When should your classroom be quiet? When should it be noisy?

Discipline and Discipleship

"And we urge you, brothers, warn those who are idle, encourage the timid, help the weak, be patient with everyone" (1 Thessalonians 5:14).

• According to this verse, what are some possible sources of misbehavior in a classroom?

• Why is patience a necessary response for any form of misbehavior?

▼ Training Session

Discipline and *discipleship*—two closely related words. Both come from the same Greek word for "to learn." So why do we see discipline as negative and discipleship as positive?

Maybe it's because, in our culture, *discipline* has more to do with control than with learning.

As a teacher, you deal with misbehavior. And you have an important choice when misbehavior arises: to control your classroom or to use the misbehavior as an opportunity for learning. Two very different goals. Control equals a quiet classroom (and frustrated students). Learning leads to discipleship.

So if the goal's discipleship, it's not enough to control a child. Instead, equip.

God's placed you here to help your children grow—emotionally *and* spiritually. It's your important job to give kids the tools they need to learn. Here's how:

- **Check *your* emotions first.** When a child misbehaves, it's natural to react emotionally. After all, the child *is* acting against you.

  But don't use your emotions to react—that just makes things worse. Respond. Use your own emotions as a clue to understand the child's emotions. A child who makes you angry probably wants control. A child who hurts you may have felt hurt *by* you or another adult.

- **Check *their* emotions.** Ask direct questions. "How are you feeling right now?" "What made you feel that way?" Ask for honesty.

- **Be honest yourself.** Tell the child how you feel—and how his or her behavior is affecting the class. Be direct, but be warm.

- **Help the child find a better behavior.** Talk about behavior that would have been more productive. Lay out some options, and let the child choose. Help kids see that one of the options isn't the behavior you're correcting.

- **Reinforce changes.** When you see children improve their behavior, point it out. They'll be glad you noticed.

Take this training deeper as you think over these questions:

- What does discipline mean to you?

- What's been the goal behind your classroom management up until now: control or maturity? Is it time to upgrade your goal?

- What are some potential challenges you'll face as you use misbehaviors as an opportunity to foster maturity?

▶ **Journal**

God, I struggle with this type of discipline challenge...

God, please give me patience when...

May God bless you and give you eternal patience. Thank you for coaching your children to maturity!

▼ Application

Write down the last few discipline challenges you've faced in the classroom. Write down who was involved and what you felt as it was unfolding. Next, write down why you think the child or children misbehaved. What emotions seemed to motivate the misbehaving?

How can you begin to teach these children how to pursue these goals in a positive manner?

Distractions

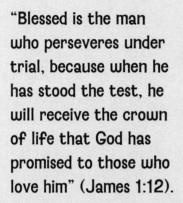

"Blessed is the man who perseveres under trial, because when he has stood the test, he will receive the crown of life that God has promised to those who love him" (James 1:12).

• How can you learn to persevere through difficult moments in your classroom?

• How do you keep focused on the main goal despite distractions?

▼ Training Session

Working with kids and their seemingly endless amounts of energy can be the greatest blessing…*and* the greatest challenge. With children's energy comes a number of distractions: blurting out questions, cracking jokes, commenting on the snow falling outside as they stare out the window.

It can be hard to stay focused on what you've set out to do—to help children grow closer to Jesus.

And you don't want to squelch their energy—just channel it.

So *match* their energy. Be energetic from the moment *before* the kids walk in the room. Exude interest in your lesson. Engage kids. You'll capture their attention—and their minds will be less tempted to wander.

Also keep in mind that a lot's happened since you last saw your kids. So allow for sharing time early in the session. If they tell their stories then, they won't need to when it's your turn. Ask questions about the week. If you have a small class, give each child a minute to tell a story to everyone. With a large class, have kids pair up to share.

Kids don't only have things to *tell* you. They also like to ask questions—sometimes right on track, many times not.

Value their questions. Your classroom is a good place to share the questions and thoughts in their hearts.

Quickly decide if the question is one to integrate into your lesson or not. If not, it's OK to say, "I love your question. Why don't we finish up here, then while we're working on our craft project, you and I can talk?" This gives value to the question but redirects the focus back to the point.

Your kids are also creative. And they love to share their creativity. Give them that opportunity at appropriate times. For example, you may have a student with a great sense of humor. He loves to crack jokes. But sometimes the jokes come at the wrong moment, distracting from your lesson.

Talk with that student one-on-one: "I want you to know I think you're very funny! I love your sense of humor, but there's a good time and a bad time for being funny. Watch me. If I'm being serious, you should be serious. If I'm more relaxed, that would be a great time for a joke."

Encourage personality growth. Provide an avenue.

Distractions are natural with kids. Give them space to tell stories and ask questions.

And give them grace to be themselves.

Take a deep breath and know that you're playing a significant role in their lives. It won't always be perfect.

And that's OK.

Take this training deeper as you think over these questions:

- Think of a recent situation in your own classroom. How can you help manage a specific child's distractions?

- Does your class time allow for your kids' creativity to be expressed?

- What would change if you were to rearrange your classroom schedule to accommodate time for questions and storytelling?

▶ Journal

Lord, help me see all the children in my class for all you've made them to be, and when they distract from what I'm trying to do...

God has trusted you with his children. The time you spend with them leaves an eternal mark. It may feel frustrating at times. But look at the big picture. You're doing kingdom work. *That* will leave an imprint on the hearts and minds of the children you serve!

▼ Application

Choose a day this week you'll count distractions. Just make note of each time you're distracted—when your attention is diverted from what you're focused on—during that day. After you do that, answer the questions below.

- How many times were you distracted?
- How did it feel?
- Were the distractions worth your being distracted? Why or why not?
- Were they important to someone else?
- How can you take what you learned from this experience and apply it to your class?

It's All About Age

> "The Lord disciplines those he loves" (Proverbs 3:12a).
>
> ---
>
> • Why do you think God disciplines those he loves?
>
> ---
>
> • When is a time you were disciplined by God? How did that change your life?

▼ Training Session

Knowing how to lovingly set appropriate boundaries and expectations is one of the greatest challenges of teaching—and one of the most necessary.

But what *can* you expect from your kids?

Is it normal for a 4-year-old to have a temper tantrum if he doesn't get as many fish crackers as his friend? Should you be surprised if fifth-grade girls act like enemies every week?

Well, 4-year-olds *do* throw tantrums every now and then. "It's not fair" is often the argument. And fifth-grade girls can be best friends one minute and worst enemies almost on cue.

Here are a few things to expect at different age levels.

Preschoolers are

- intense with their emotions. When they're happy, they'll be all smiles. When they're unhappy, they're sure to let you know.
- able to be a part of a group. But they see *themselves* first. Preschoolers play together, but don't interact much. They're not quite to the stage of sharing yet. Don't expect them to understand the concept.
- fairness filters. They'll make sure everything's fair. This is where the temper tantrum might come in.
- adult pleasers. Simply say, "I'm not very happy with the way you're acting." That'll give them something to think about.

Younger elementary kids

- like to be first. It's a pride thing. Don't play games that produce losers, and you won't see the tantrums show up.
- want to be your friend. Learn their names and some special things about them. You can reason with them on a more personal level.
- aren't ready to see things from another's point of view. When you reason with them, do it from their point of view: "How would it make you feel…"

Older elementary kids

- need approval. Validate their feelings. Applaud good behavior.
- bask in high expectations. Give them responsibility. They'll perform with excellence.
- can be reasoned with from another's point of view. Talk with them about how their actions affect the whole group.
- experience mood swings. Expect the unexpected—because it'll happen.

When you know how your kids can and can't behave, you can eliminate problems before they even occur. Set age-appropriate expectations. Make them clear. You'll quickly become a master teacher!

Take this training deeper as you think over these questions:

- How well do you know the age-level characteristics of the kids in your class?

- How can you better understand child development?

- What do you expect of your kids?

▶ Journal

Lord, please help me to see how you've designed the kids in my class.
Give me wisdom and insight as I...

It's no accident that you're teaching this particular class at this particular time. God has plans for your life and for the lives of the children you teach. Trust God to guide you as you prepare to teach.

▼ Application

Go to a library. Check out a book or two on child development. (Piaget and Erikson are good authors to start with.) Make a simple list of age-level characteristics of kids who are the same age as your students. Keep the list handy as you read through next week's lesson.

Let the Kids Decide

> "You, my brothers, were called to be free. But do not use your freedom to indulge the sinful nature; rather, serve one another in love" (Galatians 5:13).
>
> ---
>
> • When have you given children freedom?
>
> ---
>
> • How are you currently empowering your students to make good choices concerning their behavior?

▼ Training Session

A child defiantly asks, "Why do I have to sit down?" How do you respond?

"Because I said so" doesn't exactly work. Sure it'll get kids to do what you want. But what do they *learn*? Does that help kids really mature?

God gives us freedom to choose. So try this approach: Give kids choices.

Let kids choose the rules. It's great to set guidelines *with* your class. Let them have a say in the rules.

Start with a general set of guidelines, three basic concepts to lay a foundation. These usually work well:

• Respect others.
• Take care of our resources.
• Participate with enthusiasm.

These general rules cover pretty much everything. If you want to add one or two, fine, but draw the line at five. Keep things simple.

Let kids know these are your expectations. Then let them work together to define each one. For example, have elementary kids come up with five behaviors they'd expect under each guideline. If you teach preschool children, ask them how to treat each other, how to treat toys and the classroom, and what they should do during activities.

Then look over kids' definitions. Make sure they're accurate. For example, "Eat doughnuts every week" isn't a rule. "Use kind words" is.

Letting kids decide their own expectations allows them to set goals—and to have a big stake in their learning environment.

Let children choose the consequences. Sometimes even when kids set their own expectations, they don't live up to them.

It's easy to remove the misbehaving child from the environment. But that also removes learning. Rather than quickly sending children to timeout, give two or three options.

Let them choose if they want to participate: "You can either choose to participate with everyone or choose to spend time away from the group. It's your call."

Or give a choice of consequences: "You can either be my partner for this activity or spend time away from the group. You decide."

Giving the privilege of choice empowers the child to choose wisely.

If you've given choices and the child breaks a rule again, take away the privilege to choose. Say, "I'm sorry. You've been given choices and the chance to make the right choice. Now it's my turn."

When you give kids power to choose, they'll learn that they have power over their own behavior. And you won't be seen as the disciplinarian!

Take this training deeper as you think over these questions:

- Why would your children want to decide their own rules and consequences?

- How can allowing your students to decide their own consequences encourage them to make good choices?

- Coach or disciplinarian—which way are you leaning right now? Why?

▶ Journal

Lord, help me to discipline in love when I'm faced with challenges, especially as I face...

Lord, please help me be a coach by...

God wants the best for you. He created an incredible system of rewards and consequences. If you find the area of discipline a bit challenging, follow his lead. His disciplinary measures are fueled by his love for you. That's an attitude worth noting!

▼ Application

Learn by example. Pop into another class (maybe even a school classroom) to see how other teachers handle rules and consequences. How does a teacher enforce expectations? What are the expectations? Can you tell just by hanging out in the room? Do kids feel empowered? What can you take from that class to use in yours?

Power of Parents

"Therefore, my dear brothers, stand firm. Let nothing move you. Always give yourselves fully to the work of the Lord, because you know that your labor in the Lord is not in vain" (1 Corinthians 15:58).

• Do you face any discipline challenges that are hard to keep firm about?

• How is being consistent in your discipline a form of "the work of the Lord"?

▼ Training Session

When wrangling over misbehavior, you might be tempted to end the struggle once and for all by going straight to the parents. *They* can deal with it!

Before you grab that phone, consider these points. As a teacher, your role is to support faith growth at home. You need a strong *alliance* with parents. Bringing discipline problems to a parent too early might make parents discouraged—or even turn them against you.

You want to bring parents into your classroom in positive and fun ways—not just as the strong arm.

There's another damaging effect of involving parents too early in discipline. You'll undermine every other form of discipline you use! Over time, the children in your classroom will *only* respond to you when you involve a parent.

So when *do* you get the parent involved?

When you've exhausted every other appropriate form of discipline.

That last sentence is a safeguard for you. So don't push the parent button if you're just frustrated. Push it when a parent's intervention is absolutely necessary.

Your children's ministry  probably has a discipline policy that outlines the steps of appropriate correction. (If not, talk to your leader about getting one in place.)

A good policy starts with giving the child a polite oral warning ("Please…"), followed by the request being made more firmly ("Austin, I asked you to…"); it then progresses to a more serious consequence.

Only after exhausting all these steps—and realizing that enforcing consequences won't help—do you involve a parent.

In a moment of frustration, it's easy to misuse these steps as a "countdown" to ejecting the child from the classroom. That's not the goal. Coaching a child in behavior is the goal. Be aware of your emotions and motives as you discipline.

But there are times when you *need* to immediately involve a parent. If a child becomes a safety risk, go to the parents. Or if a child causes *significant* property damage (breaking a pencil in anger is minor; punching holes in drywall is not), go to the parents.

Build positive connections with parents. When kids see that you communicate with their parents, that knowledge might be enough to make them less likely to misbehave.

Take this training deeper as you think over these questions:

- How do you tend to view parents? People who dump off their children? Or potential partners? Why?

- How can you find opportunities to encourage the parents with positive behavior reports? How about spiritual growth reports? Or support?

- What steps can you take to strengthen your discipline skills so you don't feel the need to be overly reliant on parents?

▼ Journal

God, please help me honor my students' parents by. . .

I want to grow in my ability to discipline in these ways. . .

Perhaps teachers who bring parents in too soon don't trust their own discipline skills. But remember this: You have more resources for positive discipline than you might realize. You have the power to grow in your ability to discipline. And one of your greatest resources is the love you show your students. That's what makes them *want* to please you!

▼ Application

It's time to review the discipline policy of your children's ministry. What are the progressive steps to take when correcting a child?

If your church doesn't have one, this is a chance for your ministry to mature. Contact your ministry leader and let that person know that you'd like guidance in how to discipline children—including when to involve parents.

If you approach your leader with the right spirit, you'll prompt him or her to take action.

Never Let Them See You Sweat

▼ Training Session

> "A gentle answer turns away wrath, but a harsh word stirs up anger" (Proverbs 15:1).
>
> • What are some gentle answers to an angry or hurt child?
>
> • What are some words that might stir up anger in a child?

Woody Hayes was an Ohio State football legend—a coach who'd won 238 games and lost only 72. But in the last game he coached, Hayes reacted to a pass interception by literally punching an opposing player. Hard. On national television.

Hayes let his temper destroy his career.

Teachers aren't supposed to get angry and show their tempers in class… but it's tempting, isn't it? Jacob refuses to listen, Kayla insists on interrupting, and Brendan's busy entertaining instead of participating—all at once. You feel your temperature rising, your face growing red. You're not being respected— and your reaction is anger.

Be careful: You're about to go "Woody Hayes."

Hayes lost his job—and career. The damage that would result from your slamming down your Bible or erupting into a tirade would be far worse.

It might keep a child from ever returning to your classroom to learn about Jesus.

Do whatever it takes to stay silent if you're feeling the need to condemn, mock, or in any way destroy the spirit of a child—even a child who's misbehaving.

Here are four safety valves to keep handy for those moments of frustration or anger:

1. Pause and seek understanding. Tap into why you felt the need to snap. Are you nervous? Had too much caffeine? Weren't prepared for the problem? Feeling a loss of control?

2. Evaluate your goals. What were you trying to accomplish? If it's to connect with kids and communicate God's love through your words and actions, how does blowing your stack accomplish that? It won't—so pause, take a deep breath, and engage kids where they are. If they simply can't—or won't—engage with the lesson, turn things around: Ask them about their lives. Work on the relationships this week. Dive into the lesson next week.

3. Evaluate your kids' expectations. Maybe they're misbehaving because they're not getting what they expected to receive. Have you dropped games lately, or eliminated another favorite part of the routine? It's OK to ask students why they're not following the classroom rules.

4. Evaluate your expectations of yourself. You want to be an excellent teacher, and that's a great goal. Your students need an excellent teacher. But you also need to be your students' friend. Maybe your kids need a friend to ask what's behind their restlessness or rudeness, to challenge their behavior and offer alternatives. Maybe you'll need to teach your children how to learn together before they're ready to learn.

Take this training deeper as you think over these questions:

- How can avoiding losing your cool create a better teaching environment?

- What causes you to lose your cool? How can you avoid that next time?

▼ Journal

*Circle the situations below that would make your blood boil;
underline the words that would keep your temperature the same.*

- A child tells you "no."

- Two children scream at the top of their lungs as they wrestle with a toy.

- A child gets up and runs for the door.

- A child yells a curse word.

- A child tells a very off-color story.

- A child sits off to the side and refuses to join the group.

- A child uses the Lord's name in vain.

- Know of one that's not listed? Write it here:

_____

Now ask God to give you patience for those you circled.

Perfection isn't your ultimate goal. Being a character of excellence *is* the critical goal. You can do it—God will help!

▼ Application

Self-control is a fruit of the Spirit—and a good one to practice. Take a cube of ice in your hand. As it melts in the palm of your hand, consider how you can have a positive attitude in each scenario listed in the journal section above.

After two minutes, throw away the ice. Now consider how hard it was to think of *positive* things while you were distracted with physical pain. How is that like or unlike what happens in the classroom as you think of addressing problems with a positive attitude?

It's a God Thing

• When have you seen evidence of this verse in your life?

• How can you apply this verse to your ministry?

▼ Training Session

God moments. As a teacher, you have them often in your classroom. But do you actually recognize God moments for what they are?

Some might define *God moment* as a teachable moment. And it is. But that doesn't really do it justice. A teachable moment occurs when you're teaching a lesson on patience and the CD player doesn't work. You stop the lesson right there and explain that this is a situation where you need to exercise some patience. Helping kids see a practical application of what they're learning is a valuable teaching aid—a teachable moment.

But it's probably not a God moment.

A God moment might come during the same lesson, when you just happen to overhear Tiffany tell a friend that her parents are getting a divorce and she doesn't know how to handle it. It's no accident that you overheard that comment.

So what do you do about it? You can ignore it and stay on track with your lesson. You can even really comfort Tiffany, sharing in her grief, and asking if there's anything you can do. You'll make her feel valued and cared for.

But any teacher can do that. A *great* teacher takes it further.

You see, a God moment is an ordinary distraction that's taken another step: to a new level of spiritual learning. It's a teachable moment—and so much more! Ask Tiffany if she'd like to ask the rest of the class for their help in handling her feelings. If Tiffany agrees, you can involve the class in offering her their care and concern. Maybe a classmate will relate what helped him or her in a similar situation. You might have the class pray for Tiffany. Results? Tiffany's encouraged, the class has bonded, and kids exercised Christian compassion and prayer. *That's* a God moment!

We can't plan for God moments. By definition, they're arranged by God. But we *can* often overlook them.

We may think that getting through the lesson is more important than stopping and heading into uncharted territory. We may be unsure of what to say, so we say nothing at all.

But rather than overlooking God moments, be on the lookout for them. Rather than viewing those moments as distractions, embrace them as opportunities from God to draw closer to him and to the others in your class.

Take this training deeper as you think over these questions:

- What's *your* definition of a God moment?
- When have you missed a God moment in your ministry?
- When has a God moment changed your life?

▼ Journal

Lord, you are the Master Teacher. Teach me to...

You're never alone when you teach. God's right there with you. So it's logical that there will be times when he interjects a situation he can use to teach or reach someone in your class for his purpose. (And don't be surprised if that someone is you!) Open your heart to God as he uses you. After all, he's the Master Teacher!

▼ Application

Keep a journal of God moments in your life, both in and out of your classroom. Maybe it's a chance meeting with an old friend who needs a word of encouragement. Or maybe it's a time in class when the lesson needs to stop in order to attend to the needs of a hurting or confused child. The more you see God working in your life, the more you'll expect to see him!

For Such a Time as This

▼ Training Session

"There the angel of the Lord appeared to him in flames of fire from within a bush" (Exodus 3:2a).

• How does God get your attention—especially in your classroom?

• Do you think God has ever "spoken" to you while you were teaching? What happened?

God's probably never spoken to you in a burning bush, but maybe he *has* used a moment in your classroom to get your attention and get you thinking. It's important to be ready for "God moments" in your classroom. You must not be so focused on your lesson that you miss the ways God's speaking to you and the opportunities he's giving you to more deeply connect with the children in your class. Listen to this true story of a missed God moment:

Several young girls sat in a classroom cutting and gluing as they worked on a craft. The girls and their teacher were talking about the lesson when one of the girls mentioned that a family member had died just that week. The other girls whispered their apologies and offered their sympathies.

A few moments later, another girl told the class that she, too, had recently suffered the death of someone close to her. The classroom became hushed and quiet as the girls continued to work. The teacher then told the girls that a good friend of hers passed away a couple years ago.

And then, just as quickly, the teacher turned away from the girls to prepare for the next activity. And told the girls to hurry up and finish their crafts.

God was speaking in that classroom—and he was ignored. Imagine the opportunities missed in that moment—opportunities for the teacher to grow closer to the girls, and for the girls to grow closer to each other. Opportunities for all of them to talk about how God is a comforter and companion in troubled times, and to pray together as a community of faith.

As teachers, we need to be aware of moments in our classrooms when God speaks to us, trying to help us grow closer to the kids we serve—and trying to help kids grow closer to him. Of course, God moments don't always look like the one described above. Sometimes they come in the form of a child asking a silly question, an everyday interruption, a child coming to class crying about a lost pet, or a strange comment. These are all moments when we can help connect God's love, care, comfort, and presence to kids' everyday lives and problems. These are opportunities to help kids understand that God is for *all* times, not just for Sundays.

Don't miss God moments when they arise in your classroom! Imagine if Moses had ignored the burning bush: Israel might still be in bondage!

And who knows but that God has put you in kids' lives for such times as these?

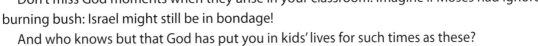

Take this training deeper as you think over these questions:

- Were there any God moments in your class last week? What were they?

- How did you respond to those moments? How could you have responded better?

- How can you become more sensitive to God moments in your class?

▼ Journal

God, help me to be more aware of God moments in my class by. . .

God has placed you in a unique position of trust and authority in your kids' lives. You have the opportunity to help children see God at work and respond to him during times of joy and trouble. Thank you for helping children recognize God as a presence in their everyday lives!

▼ Application

Write down a list of ten distractions that could happen in your class at any given time. For example, a piece of technology doesn't work, a child is obviously sad or upset, or a storm knocks out your church's electricity.

After you write your list, write down how each can be turned into a God moment. How might God speak through that situation? What can kids learn from it?

Watch for these "distractions" and turn them into God moments in your next lesson.

The Nevers of God Moments

▼ Training Session

"Some, however, made fun of them and said, 'They have had too much wine' " (Acts 2:13).

• What do you think the disciples who heard this sarcastic remark felt?

• How can our words help or hinder a child's wonder of God?

As a teacher, God has blessed you with a child's time—and special moments that only God can provide to teach children.

Kids experience life—and they wonder about lots of stuff! God brings those moments to you to help children understand—and to help them grow closer to him.

The worst thing teachers can do is squelch those God moments by correcting children's thoughts, putting off their questions, or disregarding their feelings.

Here are the "nevers" of dealing with God moments:

• **Never rephrase a child's thoughts.** This can be tempting when you want it to fit the lesson—or when you don't think the child understands. But it only teaches a child that you're not trying to understand. Instead, ask questions to draw the child out: "Can you tell me what you mean?"

• **Never rush children to finish a sentence—and don't finish their sentences yourself.** It only shortens their sense of wonder—and puts a sudden end to their discovery. You may think you know what they're trying to say (and you probably do). But let them say it.

• **Never treat your class as a lump, a mass, or a gang.** It'll block any moments of connection you could have with your class. See children individually. As friends. They need you.

• **Never force a child to decide on a plan of action too quickly.** It will only short-circuit the path of understanding. It's better to simply *wonder* why God lets something happen—to *imagine* how God responds—than to decide on a sure answer.

• **Never ignore or silence children.** Let them process. It may not fit in your lesson, but it's important to *them*. Let the lesson go. A God moment is God's lesson for now.

The moments God gives are little blessings. Use them wisely.

Take this training deeper as you think over these questions:

- What have you wondered about God—or life? Why is it important to you?

- How is that like what's important to a child?

- When has a moment passed you by? How can you treat it differently in the future?

▼ Journal

We affirm kids when we validate their comments and respond to them appropriately. Appropriately means...

▼ Application

Children have a sense of wonder that should be mirrored! Find one like theirs. Never lose it!

Write a story—it can be as short as a paragraph or as long as you want. Tell about a lesson you've learned in your life and how you learned it.

Then read your story aloud—yes, aloud. How's your story like (or not like) what happens in a child's life? How can you help children learn through their experiences? Through distractions in your classroom?

God works in unexpected ways. Expect him to.

Don't Interrupt Me While I'm Teaching

"But seek first his kingdom and his righteousness, and all these things will be given to you as well" (Matthew 6:33).

- How will seeking God's kingdom and righteousness help you be a wise and discerning teacher?

- What have you set as the primary goal of your ministry with children?

▼ Training Session

Four-year-old Kristen was fidgeting with her new name tag—concentrating more on the cute cotton-ball sheep than listening to a story about the Good Shepherd. The lesson came to a screeching halt when the name tag finally tore off and fell to the floor.

Kristen ran over to her teacher in tears—the whole class was distracted. But Kristen's teacher turned the interruption into a God moment. She picked up the name tag, removed it from sight, and said, "Kristen, did you know our Good Shepherd, Jesus, knows our names even when our name tags fall off?"

Skillfully, the teacher transformed a distraction into a teachable moment, then returned to her lesson with the smoothness of a waltz.

These God moments are brief windows of time. God opens a door—but it'll quickly close if you don't walk through right away. The moments are disguised as distractions and off-topic questions. They're hidden in interruptions.

As a wise teacher, remember that it's OK to set the curriculum aside for these moments. Don't put a God moment off to the end of the lesson. It might vanish before the lesson's over. Or you'll run out of time. You'll lose that opportunity for kids to experience biblical truth in a unique way.

If you strap yourself to a lesson, you can deadlock the learning process. Instead of feeling guilty or frustrated about a twist, respond with a desire to use the interruption as a teaching tool.

This may not come naturally at first. Being frustrated is easy—being patient and focused on faith growth is not.

But here's the good news: When you seek God's direction, the Holy Spirit *will* provide spiritual "antennae" to help you recognize—and skillfully utilize—God moments.

Sometimes the back roads, the byways off the beaten path, are the ones that lead to the most memorable places.

Take this training deeper as you think over these questions:

• How do you react to interruptions?

• How can you foster God moments in your classroom?

• What criteria will you use to discern if an interruption should take the place of the lesson?

▼ **Journal**

Lord, help me prepare for teachable moments with my students by. . .

▼ Application

Children are not an interruption to the work. They *are* the work.

Jesus always recognized a learning moment. He knew when people were ripe for learning and he didn't let the moment pass by. Read about the woman caught in adultery (John 8:1-11), the storm on the lake (Luke 8:22-25), the man with the shriveled hand in the synagogue (Matthew 12:9-13).

How did Jesus take advantage of these opportunities? What impact did such lessons have? Make a list of ways those same principles could apply to your classroom. As a weekly reminder to "watch" for God moments, set out a pair of kid's sunglasses where they'll catch your eye as you interact with your students.

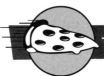

Stop! Drop! ...and Think!

"The wisdom of the prudent is to give thought to their ways" (Proverbs 14:8a).

- Why do you think it's wise to give thought to your lessons when they're over?

- How does reflection impact your future teaching?

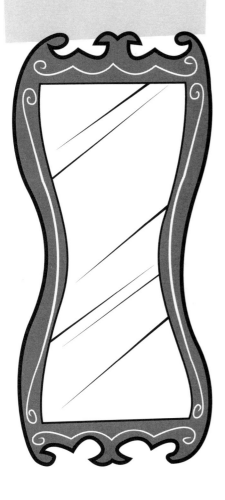

▼ Training Session

Most days after class, you probably don't even want to clean up. You'd rather rush home and move on with your life. Or maybe you need to scurry out of the room to pick up your own kids. Or you're in a hurry to get lunch out of the oven.

And that's OK. But it's important to take a few minutes—maybe while lunch is cooking or you're getting ready for bed that night—to reflect. Think about your lesson. What went well? What could have gone much, much better?

Not taking the time for reflection will make you a stagnant teacher—and your lessons redundant. If you don't evaluate your experiences, you end up reliving them again and again without ever growing or changing.

Ask yourself some questions:

- How did the class go?

- Do you feel positive or negative leaving your class? Why?

- What do you think the kids really took away from the class?

- How do you feel the kids responded to the activities? What was their favorite? Least favorite?

- Did kids give you any glimpses into how they're going to apply this lesson to their lives? If so, what were they?

Once you've answered those questions, take it a step further. Consider the implications your answers to those questions have on your classes in the future.

If you feel kids loved the obstacle course game, how can you use that knowledge as you design games in the future?

If you don't think kids understood the main point, how can you be sure they do in the future?

If you didn't see kids applying the lesson to their lives, how can you use more life-application opportunities in your lessons?

Reflection matters. A few minutes of think time will make you a master teacher and change kids' lives in new ways. So after class this week, stop, drop, and think about the experience you just had in your classroom! You'll become a better teacher if you do.

Take this training deeper as you think over these questions:

• What's the worst class you've ever taught? The best?

• Why do you feel that way about each of those classes?

• How can you avoid the things that made the worst one the worst? How can you duplicate the things that made the best one the best?

▼ Journal

I felt this way about my class last week...

God, please help me take the time this week to evaluate my class. Make me aware of the good and the bad in my class, and help me use that knowledge as I develop lessons in the future. Thank you. In Jesus' name, amen.

▼ Application

Make a list of reflection questions to ponder after your next class.

_____

_____

_____

_____

_____

_____

_____

_____

Impact Eternity

▼ Training Session

"Now that you know these things, you will be blessed if you do them" (John 13:17).

• How do you think the disciples applied the lessons they learned from Jesus?

• Do you feel that your students apply the lessons they learn in your classroom? Why or why not?

Take a moment to dream about the future of your students. Through God's power, what kind of person could each become spiritually?

It can be humbling to realize that God's using *you* as part of his lifelong process of helping children become more like Jesus. And you just thought you were teaching lessons.

Surprise! You're touching lives for eternity!

So, does your teaching make an eternal impact? Are kids applying their learning to their lives?

Application's the key to learning success. If kids can't apply it, they probably haven't really learned it. It's OK to check in with kids. See what they've learned—and how it's impacted their lives.

Here are some suggestions to find out if kids are *really* learning and growing in relationship with Jesus:

• **Give kids a weekly challenge after each lesson.** If you're teaching on serving, challenge them to serve a family member. Or have them do their chores without being asked. You can even give kids options.

• **Form accountability groups with kids.** Give them a chance each week to check in. Have them talk about what they learned the week before and how it applied to their lives.

• **Let elementary children write stories or draw pictures about what their relationship with Jesus looks like.** Give kids a question to write or draw about, such as, "How does Jesus respond when we sin?" Use their stories and artwork to gain a base line regarding their relationship with God. Repeat the exercise at the end of the year to see how they've grown.

• **Tell preschoolers to draw a picture of what it would look like if they met Jesus face to face.** Use their drawings to understand how they view Jesus.

• **Have a regular prayer time when the children can share their concerns and talk with God.** Lead the children in prayer, but also listen to evaluate how easily the children are able to talk to God.

• **When kids arrive each week, ask them to tell you some things from the previous week.** What was the Bible point? How did you see Jesus at work in your life?

Find ways to make everything you teach apply to kids' lives. When you do, you'll impact eternity in every lesson!

Take this training deeper as you think over these questions:

- Up to this point, how have you known if kids really learned?

- Can your kids summarize the point of each lesson in one phrase? Why or why not?

- How can your kids be blessed if they *do* what they learn?

▼ Journal

God, these are my highest hopes for the children I work with...

These are my fears about evaluating my lessons for application...

As you make the leap to life application in every lesson, you'll begin to see your children through God's eyes. God's goal for your kids is that they reflect his character. And by participating in God's goals, you've just become a partner with him!

▼ Application

Write down a list of all the characteristics of a child who has a growing friendship with Jesus.

Next, write down a list of how you would know that those things were actually in the life of a child. What would the child act like? What would the child's life look like?

You've just taken the beginning steps of evaluating for transformation. For extra credit, check your current curriculum's "application" section. Are children being invited into life change? If not, consider rewriting those sections, or consider suggesting to your ministry leader that it's time to go shopping.

Head Knowledge vs. Heart Change

"But the goal of our instruction is love from a pure heart and a good conscience and a sincere faith" (1 Timothy 1:5, New American Standard Bible).

• What could happen in the lives of your students if those three objectives were built into their lives?

• How do you know if you've met these goals?

▼ Training Session

As teachers, we want to make sure our lessons aren't just filling heads, but are changing hearts. You're teaching for life transformation. So at the end of a lesson, how do you know your students' lives have been transformed?

It's not an easy question—but it's an important one!

It's tempting to look at head knowledge and evaluate what kids *know*. The first thing we teachers like to test is memorization. After all, if kids can memorize a Bible verse or concept, they've surely learned *something*—right?

Well, that depends.

If a child's memorized a Bible verse to get a reward but hours later doesn't remember the verse, then no, that's not true learning.

If a child's perfectly memorized the words of a Bible verse but can't actually tell you what the verse means, then no, that's not our goal either.

If a child's memorized a verse about serving others, and then the child helps a friend pick up his or her toys, then yes, that's true learning—that's life transformation!

Our goal is for kids to be living examples of God's Word—not just recordings of God's Word!

Instead of evaluating whether or not kids know a Bible verse, gauge what it means to them. Instead of asking kids to recite the Ten Commandments, see if they can give an example of one of them.

When evaluating kids' learning, try these ideas for looking at the heart, not the head.

- **Have kids rewrite a memory verse in their own words.** And when they recite it, accept the paraphrase as correct.

- **Let kids create a visual.** Have kids act out, write about, or draw what the memory verse or Bible point looks like when it's put to work in their lives.

- **At the end of each lesson, have kids summarize in a single phrase what they learned.** Have kids write the phrase on index cards or whisper it to you as they leave.

- **Make a note each week of how you've seen a child grow.** It may be a way a preschooler shared a toy he's never shared before. Or you might see a fourth-grader start talking to her friends about Jesus more.

Sometimes gauges like these seem less concrete than Bible memorization and recitation, but these provide more than a peek into kids' brains. They're a glimpse into their hearts! And, ultimately, which is more important?

Take this training deeper as you think over these questions:

- What's the difference between memorization and learning?

- How can you make sure kids *understand* what they're learning?

- Why is it so easy to focus on head knowledge rather than heart change?

▼ Journal

What is it that I want kids to learn from this week's lesson?
How can they apply that to their lives?

God, I want to see life transformation in my students' lives. I want them to learn how to live for you and through you. Help me find ways to catch a glimpse inside each child's heart. Thank you. In Jesus' name, amen.

▼ Application

Create a Heart Monitor for your kids. Get two paper plates. Use a pen to divide both plates into four pie slices. Label the four slices on one plate the following: (1) in one ear, out the other, (2) memorization only, (3) knows the basics, and (4) true understanding!

Cut one slice out of the other plate. Use a brass fastener to attach the cut plate to the labeled plate so it covers all but one slice.

Decorate your Heart Monitor with…well, hearts! Use it to gauge your kids' learning each week. Adjust your lessons to reach for true heart transformation.

The Taste of Success

> "Finally, brothers, whatever is true, whatever is noble, whatever is right, whatever is pure, whatever is lovely, whatever is admirable—if anything is excellent or praiseworthy—think about such things" (Philippians 4:8).

• Did you succeed last time you taught? How?

• Who sets the standard of success in your class? Who else?

▼ Training Session

What's success? For a bricklayer it's a finished wall that stands up. For a mechanic it's a car that runs. For a pilot it's a safe flight. For a fashion designer it's a line of clothing that sells. For a teacher…

How do you know when you've succeeded?

A teacher's succeeded when a child's life is transformed, right?

Certainly! But you may not always see that transformation. What about some immediate results that show success? Who can wait around 20 years to see if that 3-year-old really grew into a Christ-like adult? You *can* have immediate evidence of success, and here's what to look for.

• **You succeed as a teacher when you compare who you are today with who you were last year!** Or even who you were last week! Did you grow yourself? Are you a better teacher? Did you learn from a mistake—even a success?

• **You succeed as a teacher when you develop new styles and approaches in working with children!** Are you staying on top of your game? Knowing that the goal is transformed lives, what's the best way to get kids there? Try new things. Step out of your comfort zone. Just trying is a great measure of success!

• **You succeed as a teacher if you see your students' behavior improve.** Is your classroom a laboratory of learning? When you teach kids, give them the opportunity to apply what they learn—right then and there. You know you're successful when you see them put into practice what they learn!

• **You succeed as a teacher when you pace yourself for the long haul.** If you were to teach only four lessons over and over again, you'd become incredibly good at it, wouldn't you? But at what cost? You'd lose your mind—and your students—with boredom! Don't try to become perfect. But practice those things that'll result in you wanting to *remain* a teacher. Love the role you're in, and you'll succeed.

• **You succeed as a teacher when you learn from succeeding.** What components worked to make you succeed? What will you keep? Many churches—and people—fail right after they succeed. They get caught up in the feeling of success and don't learn from what went right.

Succeed well.

Take this training deeper as you think over these questions:

- What are your strengths?

- How can you use your strengths to continue to grow?

- When was the last time you felt success? What did it feel like? What did you learn from it?

Ultimate success is found in heaven's words, "Well done, thou good and faithful servant!"

▼ Application

Spend some extra time this week preparing your heart by reading the teacher's devotion that comes with your lesson. If your lesson doesn't have a devotion, use the lesson itself to allow God to speak to you! You can't impart what you don't possess.

It's Not Whether or Not You'll Fail

> "For it is by grace you have been saved, through faith—and this not from yourselves, it is the gift of God—not by works, so that no one can boast" (Ephesians 2:8-9).

• Why do we need God's grace in our teaching?

• How should we treat failures in our teaching?

▼ Training Session

Lessons will fail. You'll fail.

Don't beat yourself up. God extends his grace in our failures—do your best to do the same for yourself.

The good news: You'll succeed lots more than you'll fail!

But when you do fail, you can learn a lot from what went wrong.

• **Ask yourself questions.** When you ask questions, you'll find the root of the failure—and you won't repeat it next time. Ask: Why didn't that work? What got in the way? What can I learn from that flop?

Unless you identify what it was that failed, you might end up doing it again. You may also identify the failure with the whole lesson—and forget about all the amazing strengths of the lesson and your teaching.

• **Respond in gentle love.** There are times where your whole plan—your lesson, your hopes for the day—will fall flat on its face. It's the nature of teaching. How you respond will end up being the real lesson that day. You're modeling Christ's love and character for children. The details of lesson plans—in success or failure—will pale in comparison to your love and gentleness.

Abandon your plan when the lesson collapses, and spend time on relationships. Play with the kids. Talk to them. You can revisit your lesson another time.

• **Talk about it.** Talk your feelings of failure over with another teacher or your ministry leader. It'll help you to hear that other people experience similar feelings of failure. You'll be able to run what happened by an objective set of ears. And you may gain some valuable insight into what to do differently.

• **Make a plan for change.** God handed you this little learning experience for a reason. Praise him for the opportunity to grow. Then grow. Do you need to prepare a little more? Or less? Do you need more of a variety of activities? Are your kids begging for a different routine? Could you handle a situation better next time?

In the end, realize it's really OK. Failure now sets you up for success later!

Take this training deeper as you think over these questions:

- When something doesn't go as planned, how can you let go of that frustration?

- How can you seek the gems of learning in the mud of failure?

▼ Journal

Lord, help me to forgive myself...

The ministry you're doing as a teacher isn't easy—and it's a job that'll send you curveballs almost every week. Children are more impacted by the time you spend with them than the perfect lesson, perfectly executed.

▼ Application

Create an emergency response plan to help you deal with failure. List steps you'll follow when a lesson or an attitude or a behavior flops.

For example, step one might be to take a deep breath. Step two could be asking God for guidance in the moment and taking action. Step three could be reflecting on what went wrong. Step four might be talking to a specific person about the problem. And step five could be an action plan to make the appropriate change.

Keep your emergency response plan handy for the next failure. Then turn failure into success.

BONUS:
Getting Feedback From Others

> "Watch your life and doctrine closely. Persevere in them, because if you do, you will save both yourself and your hearers" (1 Timothy 4:16).

- What does it mean for you to persevere in your life and doctrine?

- How does seeking guidance and evaluation from peers help you persevere in these areas?

Tell us your comments!!

▼ Training Session

It's easy to ignore the parts of our lives that need improvement. We might not know they exist. Or we know they exist—we just don't want to spend the time to do the work!

That's why we need objective opinions—other people who tell us *honestly* how we're doing. Getting feedback from others will help you grow as a teacher, will help you adapt your lessons to work better for your students, and will help your kids better grow in a relationship with Jesus.

You can seek feedback from lots of different angles:

- **Your leader.** Ask your ministry leader to come into your class and observe for a lesson—or even for only a few minutes. Agree on a set of standards you'll be evaluated on, then ask your leader to give constructive criticism. Then set a time to sit down with your leader to go over what was observed. Find out how you can grow, but make sure you know the areas you're excelling in, too!

- **Your students.** That's right! Let your *kids* tell you how they think you're doing. Make a list of topics you need them to evaluate you on—making things interesting, sense of humor, feeling welcome in class, feeling like their teacher cares, and so on. Have them rate you on a scale of one to four and comment on their ratings. Tell them this is anonymous! (If you think you'd recognize their writing, have a fellow teacher compile the results.)

- **Fellow teachers.** Ask a teaching partner or a teacher from another class to watch how you teach and work with children. Ask him or her to note one way you can improve and one thing you're doing well. Then talk about it over a cup of coffee.

- **Parents.** They usually know their kids pretty well. Ask them to write down some ways they've seen their kids grow since you've been their teacher. It'll be encouraging to see the maturity your kids are reaching! Remember it's not all you—but you do have a big part in their lives!

Your children deserve a teacher who's finding new ways to improve and grow. Thank you for taking the time to become a *great* teacher!

Take this training deeper as you think over these questions:

- What are some ways you're seeking evaluation in your teaching?

- What's a new method of review you'll try in the next month?

- What can you learn from different opinions of your teaching?

▼ Journal

Lord, the hardest part of being evaluated by someone else is...

> What can I do better? It's a hard question to ask—it's even harder to hear the answer. But when you take that answer and do that one thing better, it's great to hear, "You did it!"

▼ Application

Create an evaluation form. This could be as formal as a grade sheet or rubric. Or it could be as informal as a list of qualities you want in your teaching. Add things you see as important. Think of areas you'd like to improve, and add those. Think of things you know you're good at—put those on the sheet, too.

Think of three people you'd like to have evaluate you, and then give these sheets to those people. Set up a time in the next couple months for them to come watch you teach.

Theme Index

E-couragements

Each of the following E-couragements is included electronically in both Rich Text Format (RTF) and PDF format on the enclosed text CD. Feel free to edit these thoughts to match your ministry and the needs of your teachers. Your people will be sure to appreciate the e-couraging words!

E-couragement #1

Thought 4 the Day

Overcome Your Fear of Being Accepted by Children

If you accept them, they'll accept you.

You've already prepared your lesson, so you don't have to worry about that. You've gotten your supplies together, so that's not on your to-do list anymore. Your job now is to create an environment of love and acceptance for your kids.

Smile a lot. Get on their level. Listen to them. Have fun with them.

If you show them you care, you'll never have a reason to worry about them accepting you. It'll come naturally.

And don't worry about them not accepting you if you make a mistake. Children are the most forgiving people you'll meet. If you make a mistake, that's OK. In fact, they'll probably accept you more, because you showed your true self.

Kids love you!

"I have told you these things, so that in me you may have peace. In this world you will have trouble. But take heart! I have overcome the world" (John 16:33).

Overcome Your Fear of Mishandling Scripture

Moses had the same fear. When God told him to free the Israelites from Egypt, Moses insisted that he couldn't quite talk right—not right enough to do God justice, anyway.

But God insisted right back. Look at the verse at right to see what he said to Moses.

Picture a megaphone. A megaphone's a simple contraption designed for someone to speak through.

God has sent you to be his megaphone. He's already spoken the Truth. It's in the Bible. Now he speaks his Truth *through* you. All you have to do is trust God—and ask him to do the talking.

He will—just as he did for Moses.

"Now go; I will help you speak and will teach you what to say" (Exodus 4:12).

Overcome Your Fear of Failing to Teach Kids Well

"Nobody cares if you can't dance well. Just get up and dance" (Unknown).

This quote can be used to drive any part of life. It's motivating. It's compelling. It gets us to just do it.

Many people stay off the dance floor (or out of the classroom) because they feel they can't perform with grace and skill. But God is the Master Teacher. He's full of grace—and he has a purpose that transcends any plans you might have for your kids.

It doesn't matter if *you* think you can teach well—God thinks you *can*. He put you in this position to fulfill his purpose.

So get up and dance!

"Many are the plans in a man's heart, but it is the Lord's purpose that prevails" (Proverbs 19:21).

Thought 4 the Day

Overcome Your Fear of Disapproval

"Whatever you do, work at it with all your heart, as working for the Lord, not for men" (Colossians 3:23).

Howard Schultz loved coffee. But even more, he loved the experience of walking into a European coffee shop: a social meeting place. So he modeled his company, Starbucks, after that principle.

At first company executives didn't approve, claiming they didn't want to go into the restaurant business. But he did it anyway…because he believed in the principle.

His quote for today: "Care more than others think wise. Risk more than others think safe. Dream more than others think practical. Expect more than others think possible" (Howard Schultz).

Go and do the same in your class.

Overcome Your Fear of Kids Talking

As teachers, we like to talk, don't we? Sometimes we feel as if *we* have all the answers. Or we talk a lot because it gives us a sense of control over the class.

But God wants us to be slow to speak. Why is that?

Maybe it's because if we're talking too loud, his still, small voice won't be heard. Or maybe we should give kids a turn to talk. After all, we're trying to foster relationships.

If you're letting kids talk—to each other, to you, in groups—you're not talking too much. The talk in your classroom is just right. You're helping kids grow—spiritually *and* socially. Keep it up!

"Everyone should

be quick to listen,

slow to speak

and slow to

become angry"

(James 1:19b).

Overcome Your Fear of Not Talking Enough

Think of a wise person you know. Is it your grandfather? An older mentor? How talkative is this wise person? Does he talk a lot? Does she have something to say about everything?

Probably not. Usually when people reflect on a wise grandfather, grandmother, or mentor, they talk about that person's quiet, thoughtful character. But when those wise people *do* say something, you'd better listen—it's probably worth every word.

Don't worry about not talking enough…it's a good thing! Preach the Word. Say what you need to say. The Spirit *will* fill in the gaps.

"Preach the Word; be prepared in season and out of season" (2 Timothy 4:2a).

Overcome Your Fear of an Overwhelming Classroom

First of all, thank you!

Thank you for choosing to serve God by serving his children. Thank you for helping kids know and grow closer to Jesus. And thank you for facing that overwhelming classroom to do so.

The overwhelming classroom tops the list of fears for most teachers: What if I can't get the kids to participate instead of hang from the lights? What if the temperature is way too hot or cold? What if none of my supplies are where they need to be?

The list of what-ifs can be endless.

But you can handle the overwhelming classroom. Most of the time, none of the what-ifs will happen. And if they do, they'll *never* happen at the same time.

God has equipped you to do his work. He won't just say, "Here, take this curriculum…good luck!" He'll go with you—right by your side.

Be strong. Be courageous.

"Have I not commanded you? Be strong and courageous. Do not be terrified, do not be discouraged, for the Lord your God will be with you wherever you go" (Joshua 1:9).

Overcome Your Fear of Discipline

"The fear of the Lord is the beginning of knowledge, but fools despise wisdom and discipline" (Proverbs 1:7).

Think about a favorite teacher from your childhood. What did you love about this teacher? What did you learn from this teacher?

Now answer this question: Was the teacher a pushover? Or did he or she discipline you once in a while—even with just a verbal warning or glance?

Your children are asking for guidelines. They actually *want* boundaries. And they even want you to enforce consequences! When you discipline kids, you're helping them learn.

Don't be afraid to help kids grow. Some might be angry at the moment. No one wants to be told they're wrong! But they'll thank you for it later.

And I thank you for it now!

Thought 4 the Day

Overcome Your Fear of Burnout

Have you ever tried to get a campfire going and watched it just fizzle to a puff of smoke? You try again, and the puff returns—this time it seems to mock you as it blows away.

Sometimes teaching can be like getting a campfire going. Our spirit just seems to fizzle and fade away. We long for a new spark and fresh fuel.

This week, check your flame. What do you need in order to fan it to a full bonfire? Spend time with the fuel source. Talk to God. Open his Word.

Thank you for not letting burnout be an option. Be the flame that won't go out!

"For this reason I remind you to fan into flame the gift of God" (2 Timothy 1:6a).

Thought 4 the Day

Overcome Your Fear of Bewildered Children

Can you imagine the looks on the faces of the religious leaders, disciples, and others listening as Jesus turned their world upside down? Jesus was saying something about people who are first would be last…and the last would end up being first!

He talked about losing your life to gain it. But if you choose to keep your life, you'll lose it.

And then he said that we have to become like kids to get into heaven.

Talk about bewilderment! The looks on those faces must have been priceless!

As a teacher, you're sharing some kingdom concepts that can be bewildering, even to the most astute adult! But those seeds you're planting will grow.

You, too, might see some bewildered faces. But keep walking with your kids as their faith grows. Seeds grow. Trees bear fruit. In time they'll understand.

"I no longer call you servants, because a servant does not know his master's business. Instead, I have called you friends, for everything that I learned from my Father I have made known to you" (John 15:15).

E-couragement #11

Thought 4 the Day

Overcome Your Fear of Inadequacy

Talk about inadequacy! The disciples fought over who'd sit next to Jesus—but Jesus still served them. Zacchaeus was a sinister tax collector—but Jesus chose *his* house to visit. A little boy shyly handed over a few fish and some bread—but Jesus turned it into a feast for thousands. Saul persecuted followers of Jesus—but Jesus changed Saul's heart.

Jesus used all these people to fulfill his purpose. And he's using you!

You've been given a gift to teach children. You're in this place and time for a reason. Yes, you're inadequate…but everyone is! God *will* give you what you need. He won't let you fail. Children are worth too much to him.

You're worth too much.

"Not that we are competent in ourselves to claim anything for ourselves, but our competence comes from God" (2 Corinthians 3:5).

Overcome Your Fear of Looking Foolish

Have you ever stood up on a desk and danced around? Do you dress up in funny costumes to make a point? When you do motions to the songs, is your energy level higher than your kids' energy level?

If you answered no to all of these questions, maybe you're not looking foolish *enough*!

Jesus meant every word when he told us to become like children (Matthew 18:3). Wonder like children. Be innocent like children. Play like children. Have fun like children. Be foolish like children.

Children love it when we delight in them. Don't be afraid of foolishness. After all, what is there to be afraid of? No one's opinion is worth more than the smile of a child.

Today, find a way to be a fool for Christ!

"We are fools for Christ" (1 Corinthians 4:10a).

For more **amazing resources**

visit us at **group.com...**

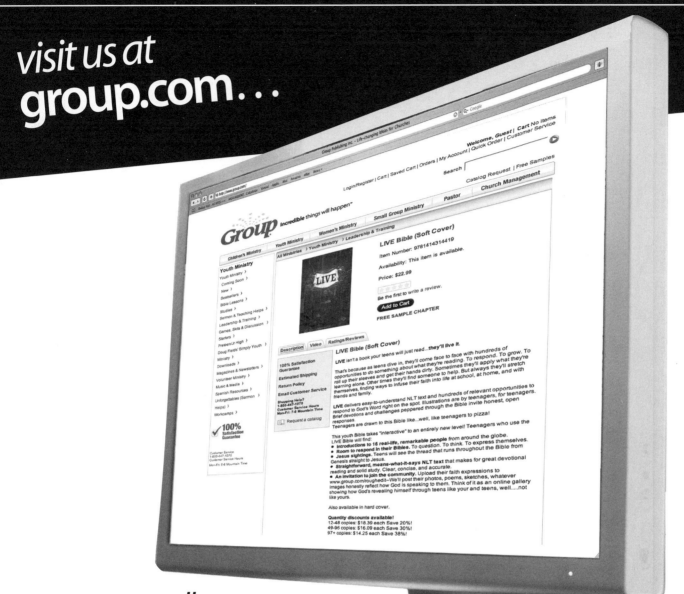

...or call us at **1-800-447-1070!**